The Story of
PAUL SMITH
Born Smart

The Story of
PAUL SMITH
BORN SMART

by
Helen Escha Tyler

Edited by
Martha Tyler John

Illustrated by
Bruce John

Published by
North Country Books, Inc.
18 Irving Place
Utica, New York 13501-5618

THE STORY OF PAUL SMITH
Born Smart

Copyright © 1988
by Martha Tyler John

ISBN 0-932052-65-7

Library of Congress Cataloging-in-Publication Data

Tyler, Helen Escha.
    Born smart: the story of Paul Smith/by Helen Escha Tyler;
edited by Martha Tyler John: illustrated by Bruce John.
        p.   cm.
    Bibliography: p.
    ISBN 0-932052-65-7: $12.95
    1. Smith, Paul, 1825-1912--2. Businessmen--United States--
Biography. I. John, Martha Tyler.--II. Title.
H.C.102.5.S5T95   1988
647--dc19   88-19493
(B)   CIP

Published by
North Country Books, Inc.
Publisher—Distributor
18 Irving Place
Utica, New York 13501-5618

Contents

Preface

Born Smart was researched and written by my mother during the last decade of her life. One of her requests just prior to her terminal illness was that we finish the book.

When I reviewed it, I found it to be an absorbing story. However, the latter portions of the book required considerable organization and repetition needed to be deleted. I have provided titles, organized chapters and done the general editing, but the script is almost wholly Helen Tyler's writing.

My sister, Phyllis Tyler, and I have both searched for bibliographic references. Mom researched in many places, in a number of libraries, read much and talked to many knowledgeable people about Paul Smith. We have found only limited references to quotations, not her complete list of resources. I know these should be provided with any book. It is our sincere hope that the reader will forgive this lapse of proper referencing, and that you will enjoy the story of this most unusual man.

—Martha Tyler John

CHAPTER I

The Beginning of a Legend

It was the summer of 1825, and life went on quietly, as usual, in the small community of Milton, Vermont.

August 20th rolled around, and with it a change came to the home life of one of the chief men of the village; a son was born that day to Phelps Smith and his wife, Marilla. The Smiths already had a two-year-old son by the name of Lewis, but this second son was more than welcome, and he was given the "high-sounding" name of Apollos Austin. Eleven years later a baby girl, who was to bear the name of Sarah, was added to the family.

As one might suppose, without using too much imagination, it wasn't long before the name "Apollos" was shortened to "Pol." In the course of time "Pol" was more often spelled "Paul." Thus it was that he, who had been christened "Apollos Smith," received the name by which he was later to become known to the world, "Paul A. Smith." He, himself, used the name so naturally that during the years to come, when about to sign some legal paper, he often had to take a second to remind himself that he had been christened "Apollos" and must so sign himself.

Paul Smith, as we shall call him, had a good sturdy New England heritage and up-bringing. Phelps Smith was a lumberman and quite likely took his sons to the woods with him while they were still small boys. Without a doubt he taught them to use a lumberman's tools, how to use a gun, how and where to set traps for the various fur-bearing animals such as muskrat, beaver, otter and foxes and the best method for catching different species of fish. Paul seemed to have been born with a love for the forest, and liked to wander through the woodland watching and studying every aspect of life.

Besides being a lumberman, Phelps Smith also owned a mill, or mills, where he had machinery for both the sawing of logs and the grinding of grist. Therefore, he not only dealt extensively in the buying of logs and the selling of lumber, but also ground grain such as wheat, buckwheat, corn and rye for his farmer neighbors. It has also been said that Phelps Smith operated a stage line known as the Red Bird Stage Line which carried the mail and probably passengers between Burlington, Vermont and Montreal, Canada. With all his enterprises he must have done fairly well and had money to invest, for we are told that some years later, "Mr. Smith lost money in the Vermont Central Railroad."

It is to be expected that young Paul, as well as his brother, helped with the work at the mills, as well as in the woods and around the home. In those early days when machinery was scarce, and most work was done by hand, every boy and every girl was taught early to share in whatever needed doing.

School Days

Paul attended the village school somewhat irregularly. School attendance was not required and the call of work, hunting, fishing, or just plain "don't want to go today," could cut the days at school to a very low number. It was hard to sit quietly at a desk, struggling to get some sense from the printed page, while the whole outside world was calling. However, in spite of his many absences and his divided attention when in school, Paul did manage to get some formal education.

For a number of years a family by the name of Washburn owned and lived on property adjoining the Smith land. They had a son about Paul's age, by the name of Hiram. The two boys were good friends and that friendship lasted through the years. Paul always called his friend "Harm" which never seemed to bother Hiram.

Not too long after his 10th birthday, Paul and Hiram decided to set about finding themselves a job. Their first paying jobs away from home took them approximately four miles due west to the shore of Lake Champlain.

Years at the Lake

At the Lake, the boys hired out to work for the Northern Transportation Line. This was a merchants line of canal boats which plied the length of Lake Champlain, passed through the Northern Canal to the Hudson River and eventually, by the way of that same river, on south to New York City. (At that time Peter Comstock, who later had much to do with the early settling of Franklin

Falls, New York was in charge of transportation on the canal.)

On the south-bound trip the canal boats were loaded with grain, lumber and other produce raised in the northern area which would be in demand in the towns and cities to the south. On the return trip the boats carried all types of merchandise, especially that desired by the northern merchants to stock their stores.

The people living to the west of Lake Champlain in New York State also made good use of the canal boats. For a few years, even farmers living as far away as Hopkinton made a specialty of raising beef cattle for butchering and shipping to the south. (Hopkinton is approximately 65 miles to the west - as the crow flies - and a little to the north from Port Kent which was then the shipping point for that area of eastern New York.)

Every fall, as soon as it appeared that continuous below freezing weather had arrived, the butchering began. All through the area the work went on almost day and night until finished. The beef was loaded onto "jumpers," which were like large home-made, wooden-runnered sleds. They were usually from eight to twelve feet long, wide enough for the six, eight or ten-inch in diameter runners to run freely in an ordinary farm sleigh track. The floor of the jumper was from 15 to 18 inches above the surface of the road.

The team used for hauling those loads of beef was very likely to be a yoke of oxen. Those teams were quite apt to be butchered at Port Kent and sent on south with the rest of the beef. Only enough oxen for making the trip home were kept. That number depended on how many jumpers were needed to transport the previously ordered merchandise, which awaited their coming, back to Hopkinton and how many men there were who would want to ride at least part of the way. The extra jumpers could be abandoned for timber was plentiful and cheap and a jumper was not hard to build.

After Paul had worked on the canal boats for a couple of years, he and his brother built a boat of their own and operated that for the next five years. It took between one and two weeks to make the round trip from the home port to the south and back again. Paul enjoyed the work and in his later life, when thinking and speaking of those years, often said, "Those were the happiest, most carefree years of my life."

The Call of the Wild Adirondacks

Paul's work on the canal boats gave him a chance to see, from a distance, quite a bit of the country as they slowly passed. Perhaps it was because of the days spent in his father's woodland as a boy that what he could see of the Adirondack Mountain area so interested him.

Besides the freight that was carried on the boats, there were also many passengers, and the boys had the chance to meet many men from all walks of life. Among them was a Captain Nat Tucker of Burlington, Vermont, who was an avid hunter. He apparently took a liking to the boys and one fall, as soon as the boats were put up for the winter, he invited Paul and Hiram to cross Lake Champlain and spend a few weeks hunting with him in the Adirondacks. They put up at the home of John Merrill, who was among the first of the Vermonters to move to New York State. He and his family had settled two or three miles to the southeast of a beautiful little body of water which became known as Loon Lake. The locality where John Merrill lived soon became, and still is, known as Merrillsville.

It appears that up to that time the boys did not see any deer, though it does not seem possible. Anyhow, the story used to be told that "Harm" asked John if there were any deer around and what they looked like. John replied that deer looked something like a calf with horns and held up his spread-out fingers to serve as horns. Hiram decided to see if he could find one and picked up his gun and went off by himself, stealing through the woods on tip-toe.

He was gone so long that John and the others got worried about him and, in late afternoon, went out looking and calling for him. Just before dark Hiram answered them.

John called back, "Did you get a deer?"

There was no answer to that, but when they came up to him they saw a dark object lying flat at his feet. "Harm" had killed a "deer" all right, but it had no branching horns and a closer look showed that it was John's best calf.

The Mountains Drew Him Back

After his first trip to the Adirondacks, Paul went back every fall as soon as the boating job was finished for the year. For some reason the untouched wilderness of those mountains on the western side of the lake had a great fascination for him. On each of

those expeditions, as he acquired a more i*
the region, his love for the area increased.

Each fall Paul stayed at the "Merrill's
small, served through a number of years
people traveling back and forth on the i*
came part of the old Port Kent-Hopkinton Turn*
pike of the early 1800's had small resemblance to the tur*
today. Due to the fact that most of the traveling was done on foo*
or with oxen, such hotels as John R. Merrill's House were to be
found about every seven miles along the route. The buildings in
those years were small and fairly certain to be made of logs. The
food was good and the beds, at worst, were a place to stretch out
on. These places also provided a stopping place where a hunter or
fisherman could put up for a few days, or longer, while he enjoyed
the relaxation to be found in the sport of his choice.

Most of the men who came to the Adirondacks in those days
were from large cities such as Boston, New York, Philadelphia
and Washington. Many of them were lawyers, doctors, politicians,
stock brokers or railroad men. They had plenty of money at their
disposal, and all of them wanted to find the very best spots to
catch the most fish or to shoot the largest deer. It was not long
until the men discovered that Paul Smith knew where some of
those spots might be. They began to hire him as a guide on their
expeditions and he was soon in great demand for that work.

Paul Smith apparently had an exceptionally pleasing personality, even when he was young. The men whom he guided took a
great liking to him and soon began to urge him to quit the canal
boat work. They wanted him to set up a place of his own where he
would be owner and proprietor and where he could take in
boarders. He would still be able to work as a guide, but he would
be guiding his own boarders. The men were sure it would be a
better paying proposition than the part-year work on the canal
boats, and the still smaller part-year work of guiding that he was
doing then. It all sounded reasonable and desirable to Paul and,
after thinking it over for awhile, he decided to try it.

Adirondack Home

Consequently, in 1848, he crossed over into New York State
with plans to make it his future home. There he rented, for a
period of three years, several acres of land locally known as the
"Lovering Place." This place was already in use as a small wayside

inn and was suited to Paul's purpose. It was there that he kept his first hotel, or "Hunter's Home" as he named it. How many boarders came is not known, but they *did* come. And they filled the hours with fishing, hunting or just roaming the woodlands. The evenings and stormy days were for visiting and, perhaps, for playing a few games of cards.

As had been planned, Paul served as guide for his own boarders and the men, as before, found him not only a number one guide, but an excellent companion and friend as well. He was witty, a "good talker" and, though he liked to talk, he liked to listen to others also. He liked to joke and enjoyed it even when a joke sometimes "back-fired" on him.

A Guide Has Many Jobs

Paul Smith was also an excellent story-teller. The peaceful, restful hours spent around the open-hearth fire while a storm raged outside; the "lazy" evening hours around that same hearth after the last chores were done, following a busy day in the woods, were enjoyable to all. The hours spent around the campfire on the shore of a lake or pond or beside a rippling stream became unforgettable times. This was because of Paul's own story-telling, and his ability to get his companions to "open up" and take part in conversational fellowship. These so-called "quiet" times were considered just about the best part of every day.

Not too long after Paul Smith had settled at Loon Lake as a "hotel keeper," he made a trip to Malone. He was just beginning to get acquainted in Franklin County and, as people began to know him, they liked him. From the beginning they liked his stories and his dry, sometimes seemingly pointless jokes.

It was more than thirty miles from Paul's Hunter's Home to Malone. A trip to Malone necessitated an over-night stay, probably two nights, if one had much business to attend to, for the traveling itself took the greater part of a day each way. Hence, there was a chance for getting acquainted and having a time of good fellowship at one's stopping place in the evening.

On one of these trips Paul found there were quite a number of men gathered at the Franklin Hotel and the subject of conversation turned for a while to fast horses. Just about every man there had a story or two to tell of horses they had owned or known. There was much laughter and everyone seemed in a good, friendly mood. Paul listened for some time and finally said, "Let *me* tell you about a horse I owned when I lived at Georgia Bridge in Vermont. He would go *any*where I wanted him to in the afternoon," and Paul stopped. There was a great volume of laughter at the abrupt ending of the story. When all was quiet again Paul added dryly, "That wasn't all. He would go home again in the evening." And the men were off again.

While Paul was renting the Lovering Place, his father and mother came to New York State and worked with him, at least part of the time. His mother was a splendid cook and, from the very first of his hotel-keeping Paul had two very important things going for him, his mother's excellent cooking and his own ability as a guide and entertainer. A great part of the reputation of Paul's hotel was based on those two characteristics and that reputation was never lowered through all the years.

CHAPTER II
Hotels Are Where Friends Meet

Paul Smith liked hotel keeping and desired to own his own place instead of renting. In 1852 he bought about 200 acres of land in the area where he was renting for a little less than $1.00 an acre. The land was located in a sheltered ravine along the North Branch of the Saranac River, approximately a mile from the shore of Loon Lake. There were swamps and bogs, hills and hollows, brooks, ponds and lakes all 'round and about, close enough to allow for a few hours of hunting or fishing most any hour of any day. The whole Adirondack area must have been a veritable wilderness in those days before the first-growth timber was cut or burned off.

Paul had the land, but no building. So he chose a spot on the north side of the stream, not far from the bridge that carried the "turnpike" across the river, and there he built his own hunter's home. Although the buildings have been gone for many years the area still bears the name that Paul gave to his first hotel, "Hunter's Home."

The hotel that he built was a simply planned wooden building. There was a large living-room and a kitchen on the ground floor. The second floor was divided into eight or ten small, thinly partitioned rooms which were to be the bedrooms for his guests.

No plans were made for women guests. It is safe to assume that neither Paul, nor the men who had urged him into the venture, ever thought that here was a woman anywhere who would care to live without the so-called conveniences, comforts and luxuries of daily living. Therefore, no plans were made for them. His first plan for a hunter's home appears to have been just that—a rustic home or camp where the men could eat, drink, sleep, rest, play games or swap stories between hunting and fishing trips.

By early spring of 1853, Paul had his building sufficiently finished to live in and he wanted to move into it before the ice went out of Lake Champlain, there being no bridges across the lake in those days. His home town of Milton, Vermont lay almost directly to the east across the lake from Plattsburgh with Grand Isle laying about mid-way between the shores of the two states.

Moving in for Good

Later, in telling how he came to New York State to live, Paul said, "I would go to the Adirondacks hunting in the fall after the boat had been put up for the winter. I went to John Merrill's place at Loon Lake at first. It was wild and rough, and there were no railroads. There was no settlement west of Loon Lake."

"I visited the Merrill place several years in the fall, and finally got ready to open Hunter's Home near Loon Lake."

"I got a pair of horses and drove from Loon Lake to Platts-burgh. I left the horses on Cumberland Head (a point of land near Plattsburgh) and went to Grand Isle. It was about the first of April and the ice was going out, but I hired a man who lived on the island to take me to Milton on the other side of the lake. The man had a little bit of a pony. We loaded some furniture on the sled (supposedly a light farm sled) and my sister, Sarah, and I started for Grand Isle. We made Grand Isle all right, but the ice was breaking up and the man with the pony wouldn't go any farther."

"I put what things we could manage on one sled and started, with my sister, for Cumberland Head. I had to leave Sarah on the ice while I went ashore and got a rope. Then, with the help of the rope, we jumped from one cake of ice to another, dragging the sled and so we got to the shore."

"And that's the way I moved to New York State."

Paul may have made the moving sound very simple, but there was certainly more to it than that, for he had to get the rest of his goods from Grand Isle and then get them all home to Loon Lake. Having gotten his sister and part of his goods safely to the New York State side, it is sensible to suppose that he went back before many hours to Grand Isle for the rest of the goods. Even though the ice was breaking up, a change in the direction of the wind could have changed the movement of the ice making it impossible for Paul to make the return trip to the island and back. It is certain that he moved from Cumberland Head to Loon Lake on sleighs for, when he was somewhere near Union Falls, the whiffletree on his sleigh broke. Of course he couldn't go on without one, so he called at the nearest home, which proved to be Isaac Fadden's and asked to borrow a whiffletree.

Isaac wasn't at home and Mrs. Fadden was a little dubious about making the loan to a stranger. But Paul explained his need again, told her who he was, and promised that he would surely bring it back if she only would loan it to him, which she finally did.

When Isaac returned home his wife told him about the stranger who had stopped to borrow a whiffletree.

Isaac said, "Who was he?"

His wife replied, "He said his name was Paul Smith. He's moving from Vermont to Loon Lake, and he promised to bring it back soon."

The name apparently meant little or nothing to Isaac. His faith in the promise of a stranger seemed very small for he told his wife, "You will never see that whiffletree again." However, much to Isaac's surprise, Paul did return it just as he had promised.

From the very first, Paul Smith's Hunter's Home was a success. During the years he operated the canal boats, he had made business acquaintances in New York City whom he now contacted and he was shrewd enough to advertise his Hunter's Home in the city papers. From the very early days of his catering to hunters, a great number of his guests were men of affluence and power in the world of business; they recommended Paul's hotel to friends of their own kind.

Simple Country Life

Life was very simple at Hunter's Home, and thus very different than his guests were used to. Perhaps that was what gave his place its greatest charm. And the place *was* homelike, made so by his sister who, though 11 years younger than Paul, kept the house and did the cooking until their parents joined them later on. Their mother then took over the cooking and housekeeping. No mention is made of it, but it is supposed Paul's father attended to the outside chores around the place, such as getting water, fire wood, etc. With his family's help and interest Paul was left free to guide and entertain his guests. Mrs. Smith was a splendid cook, and anyone who had ever eaten a meal she had prepared was more than glad to eat there again.

Though the food at Paul's was of the best, it was still plain "country" or "back-woods" fare. Venison, lake trout, brook trout, partridges or wild ducks were almost daily added to the bill of fare, along with the farm-raised foods of ham, beef, chicken, vegetables, home-made bread and pastries, butter, milk and cream, as well as coffee and tea. There were no fishing and hunt-ing laws in those days or, if there were such laws, they hadn't reached the Adirondack wilderness region yet. One could fish or hunt all the year around and there were no limits on the amount, or size of fish one was allowed to catch, nor on the game that one might kill. Paul was credited with having killed as many as sixty deer in one year.

So it was that even in those early years Paul Smith's place of business was noted for its fine meals. And the price of board and room was only $1.25 a day.

If a man desired a guide to take him into the woods to fish or hunt, the fee was $2.00 a day for the guide's services. At first Paul served as guide for all his guests, but as his guests increased in numbers he had to find other men to do some of the guiding, for no one man can go it two opposite directions, with two different parties, at the same time. Many of the men who came to Paul's wanted him and no one else to guide them. Such demands were not made entirely because of his great familiarity with the woods or his ability to take the men to a place to catch fish or kill the game they wanted. Much of the cause of their demands was the fact that they liked Paul and his kind of companionship for he was a most likeable person. He was one of the "old time Yankees," tall and athletic, raw-boned with no superfluous flesh, muscular, yet gentle. The merry twinkle in his blue eyes showed that he was full to the brim with Yankee good-humor. One writer in the late 1800s described Paul Smith as being "every inch a Yankee of the best type." He was tall and strong and was said to be handsome; his hair was yellow and there was almost always a merry twinkle in his blue eyes. He had a wide forehead, a fine face and the hands of a gentleman. His laugh was rare but hearty and his voice was musi-cal with a tone of gravity. He had a sort of lazy-streak in his gait which must have been natural for Paul used to say of himself, "I have always been a lazy man." And truth to tell, it used to be said that he "was at his best when, stretched at full length with his feet to the fire and smoking his pipe, somebody else was doing the work while he talked."

Paul also had the reputation of being the best shot with a rifle, the best paddler of a canoe, and the best concocter of "forest stew" of anyone in the region. Add to all that his talent for telling delightful stories, his keenness and the fact that while being com-panionable he was still rather reserved and reticent. All these characteristics, and many more, made up a personality that was so attractive and likeable that those who met him just once wanted to know him better.

It is doubtful if Paul Smith ever realized that it was mainly his own personality—just the fact that he was what he was—that made his venture into the hotel business such a success. One would have said that no one who could afford better would be very likely ever to stop at a place like Hunter's Home. But stop they did. Men high up in the business world—doctors, lawyers, railroad men, men of great renown and of great wealth came to Hunter's Home and wore the rough clothing that was needed in such a back-woods place. They ate and enjoyed the plain woodsman's fare. These men not only came once, but they came back year after year to this place that had no luxuries or conveniences. There was no electricity, and the rooms were lighted by candles or kerosene lamps and lanterns. There was no running water, except in the river close by. There were no bathroom or toilet facilities, except for the common washbasin or bowl, and the little square building at the end of the short path back into the woods.

A Drink Between Friends

Many of the guests who came to Hunter's Home were accustomed to an occasional drink of liquids that were stronger than tea, coffee, milk or mountain-spring water so, as the place increased in popularity, Paul decided he needed a bar. The main drink of this sort to be had around the north woods in those early years was rye whiskey, which was then selling for nineteen cents a gallon.

It took very little remodeling to install a bar. The only carpentry needed was to strengthen the floor in a corner of the large living room. A barrel of rye whiskey (31½ gallons) was laid lengthwise on the floor with the bottom end slightly raised. The bottom of the barrel was of course determined by the fact that the opposite end—the top—contained the bung-stoppered hole through which the barrel had been filled. As the barrel lay on the floor a hole approximately an inch and an eighth in diameter was bored in one of the upper-most barrel staves, near what was to be the bottom of the barrel. That done, a spigot, which is a hollow wooden plug with a wooden faucet in one end, was fitted into the newly-made hole in the barrel stave. The barrel of whiskey was then up-ended and set in place on the little platform.

As this was to be a "serve yourself" bar, the only thing still needed was something to drink from, and that need was supplied when a shiny new tin dipper was brought forth. One end of a strong cord was stapled to the top edge of the wooden barrel and the second end was securely tied to the dipper handle. Of course the string was cut sufficiently long enough to allow the dipper to be held handily under the faucet, and then to the patron's mouth as he stood to drink. The top of the barrel made a good parking place for the empty dipper.

When the bar was ready for use every man served himself by holding the dipper under the faucet and drawing whatever amount of liquor he might feel that his thirst required. The top of the barrel also served as cash register. Each man dropped his "four coppers" or cents (which was the price of a drink) onto the barrel top along with the many others usually to be found there. This bar proved to be very welcome and successful, and served its purpose for a number of years.

And A Lively Tale

It has been mentioned that Paul Smith had a great ability for, and a great delight in, entertaining an audience, either large or small, with an appropriate story. Some of Paul's stories were true and some were of the "tall story" variety based on tales he had been told and on incidents that he had seen. As time went on the stories he seemed to enjoy and told most often were of the doings and peculiarities of some of the men for whom he had served as guide. It was always of great interest to him to see how men would act, or react, to various things that happened about the hotel or on their hunting expeditions.

As time went on, Paul had a rich store of incidents to draw his stories from, for all sorts of men came to Hunter's Home. Most of the men knew well what it meant to live and hunt in a mountain wilderness. There were others who, not knowing what it would be like, came to see what they could see and to get all the fun possible out of the trip. Still others came to Hunter's Home with equipment for living in a fashionable resort such as Saratoga Springs was years ago, at the height of its fame. At least one such guest came to Paul's in those early years who was especially foppish, yet, despite that, wanted to be credited with visiting all the popular places of the day. He was determined to go, with Paul as his guide, on a rather extensive hunting trip, but refused to leave any of his "comforts" at the "Home." We shall let Paul tell about the trip a little later.

Sometimes in the years to come Paul would tell about the early days of the hotel, when the dining table was in the kitchen and when venison or trout were the principle meats served. As there were no waiters or waitresses, the men either came to the stove with their plates or Paul's mother, who was doing the cooking, would take the "spider," or frying pan, to the table. As she passed along behind the men, she would stop and ladle a helping of meat onto each man's plate. When he got that far in his reminiscing, Paul was very likely to remember one of the times when they had a change of meat for a few days.

It was in the fall of either 1854 or 1855 that Mr. R. S. Brown and a couple of friends stopped off at Hunter's Home for a short visit. When they arrived, Paul seemed in especially good humor. Upon inquiring the reason for his jollity, he told them, "Why nothing much! Only we've just been having a pig shoot." One of the men answered, "A pig shoot! What's that? What sort of a thing is a pig shoot?"

Laughing heartily, Paul replied, "I can't rightly say that I ever heard of one either, but anyhow we had one. You see we've got a couple of young fellows stopping here and I reckon they was gettin' a little tired of the quietness around here and got to hankerin' for a livelier afternoon. Anyhow they come to me upwards of an hour ago and wanted to know if there wasn't somethin' they could do that would be fun. I was tryin' to think of somethin' when they saw a middlin'-sized pig of mine runnin' around the yard out here. Soon as they saw it they thought it would be fun to shoot at the pig. And they said if I would take the pig off a little ways, and hitch it to a tree they would give me 25 cents for every shot they took at it. Well, I thought that sounded kind of hard on the pig, but my second thought told me the pig didn't stand in too much danger, considerin' the sort of shootin' they've been doin' since they've been here. And we *are* gettin' short of meat, so it wouldn't matter too much if they killed it."

"So," continued Paul, "I hunted up a rope, and caught the pig. Then I strapped it to that tree over there, with its rump toward the fellers. And they begun firin'. Of course the pig didn't like bein' hitched up, and he squealed plenty because of that. Every time a gun went off it would squeal again about one key higher than it was doin' before. But when a bullet would happen to hit the tree, or in the ground real close to the pig he would open up full blast."

"Those fellers," he said, "shot 23 times before they even touched the pig, and then they only creased it a little. So," he added, "I got $5.75 for their fun. And I've still got the pig."

Just a few minutes later the stage drove in, and Paul gave the money he had gotten from the "pig shoot" to "Uncle" John Wiley, the stage driver, and asked him to bring him some beef on his next trip up from Malone.

Paul Smith used to like to tell a story about a man who came to the hotel one summer. This man loved firearms, and he loved to shoot, but he was noted for his inability to hit the target. However, he was a good sport and seemed to enjoy all the jokes that were made about his poor marksmanship as well as did those who made the jokes.

Many days passed pleasantly, and then he asked Paul and several of his friends to go with him as he had something to show them. They followed him as he led the way to the boat house and pointed to a target up on the corner of the building just below the eaves. The amazing thing about it was that there was a bullet hole exactly in the center of the bull's eye; the man was so exultant as he told them that he was "standing 500 yards away when he fired the shot."

The men were all properly impressed and rejoicing with him because he had finally done it, when one of them who was a little more skeptical than the rest said, "That's great! But how did you manage to do it?"

"Oh!" he said, "'twas easy. I fired the bullet into the wall at 500 yards, and then I painted the target around the hole." Then they all had a good laugh at the joke he had played on them.

Other Lively Tales

From the very beginning of Paul's Hunter's Home, a great part of the attraction of the place for the guests was Paul himself. Wherever he might seat himself he was not likely long to be alone, for guests, guides, neighbors, even the hired help (if not busy) were sure to gather around him. And it was never long before Paul was started at his favorite occupation of story-telling. Paul Smith's stories revealed a little about the customs and characteristics of some of the people who were his neighbors.

Scarcely a day passed at Paul's hotel without a story-telling session during some part of the day or evening. Many stories originated in those sessions, as did the following.

One evening, late in August, a group of guests were gathered in the living room when one gentleman said, "Joe, *Fat* Joe actually climbed St. Regis Mountain!"

"Joe? Not him!" another guest replied.

"He didn't? Why he said he did!" responded the first man.

"Oh, yes, that's true! He did say so. But in July when he got back from his tramp, he told us he had walked over to the foot of the mountain. It was *since* then that he went to the top. But he didn't *climb* up. He just *lied* himself all the way to the top."

Jug-er-rum

A freckle-faced boy was sitting on a bridge over in the town of Chateaugay. He was busy baiting his fish-hook with a little green frog when Paul Smith came driving by. He stopped his horse and said, "What makes those queer noises that I hear?"

The boy stopped to spit on his bait, and then he said, "Them's bull frogs, mister."

The stranger said, "H'm'm! Is that so? Are they croakin' 'Jug-er-rum! Jug-er-rum!' like they say they do?"

The boy spit on his bait again, and replied, "No, *sir!* They wouldn't be 'lowed to croak 'Jug-er-rum' 'round here. This here is a no-license town."

Lost Watch

There's all kinds of folks come into these mountains. Just last summer a red-haired man, with a perky line of red hair along his upper lip stopped in and hired a guide boat for an hour.

He rowed out a ways in front of the boat house and just cruised around out there, real aimlessly, for the most of the hour. And then all of a sudden he pulled for the boat house, straight and fast. As soon as he got in hailing distance he begun yelling at the guides that he could see sitting around on the landing. And he was shouting, "I've lost my watch overboard!"

"Where?" they shouted back.

The boatman finished the distance to the boat landing, and then he pointed to a newly-made cut in the rim of the boat, and said, "Right here. I cut a notch right where it went over."

It Needs a Bit of Work

When telling his story of the beginnings of his hotel-keeping, Paul Smith would tell his listeners that his Hunter's Home had a very shabby look about it, that there was not a line of beauty in the crudely built, two-storied, ten-roomed, L-shaped, unpainted building. Unpainted mainly because of lack of money for paint. He would also tell of the field at one side of the building that had been burned over, where he and his father had planted potatoes among the charred stumps. Along the front of that field there was a "root fence" meaning, one would suppose, that it was the old-style stump fence that came to be so prevalent in some areas of the Adirondacks. The lumbermen of that day usually cut a tree off about three feet above the ground — actually at whatever height was right for each man to stand straight while chopping — leaving the fields dotted with stumps of that height.

Someone came up with the idea — accidentally, perhaps, to turn the stumps over onto their sides, so that the mass of roots stuck out at all angles, and to lay those stumps in as even a line as possible, all pointing in the same direction, with the roots inter-locking each with its neighbor. They made an impreganble fence that would discourage almost any creature larger and less agile than a cat to even try to get through, over, or under it.

Getting Ready for Camping

When thinking back to those early days of "guiding," and trying to make the "modern man" realize what the job of guiding entailed, Paul would start in by telling about the camping "kit" which the guide usually packed into a canvas bag — there being no waterproof bags in those days. Of course, there must be cooking utensils: a frying pan, a kettle, a ladle which could do double duty as a server of food at meal times and a container in which to melt lead for the making of extra bullets. Forks and spoons were a luxury and added extra weight to the pack so were often left behind. There must be a generous portion of hard bread, flour, coffee, sugar, a middlin'-sized piece of salt pork and pepper and salt each folded into bits of newspaper. Quite often a length of rope was also tucked into the bag. Someone in the party must carry an axe. Each man must have his own large-bore rifle which he would carry over his shoulder. If the rifle happened to be one of the old muzzle loaders, he would have to take bullets and firing caps, along with extra bits of lead he might have to melt into bullets and a bullet mold. His powder horn could be attached to his belt, as could his large knife which served for skinning deer, dressing fish and as a hatchet for cutting small brush. The knife also served its purpose well in the kitchen or dining areas where it sometimes filled in for fork or spoon.

Each man generally wore a warm flannel shirt with many pockets, corduroy trousers, large heavy boots and a slouch hat. Slung on his back was a rolled wool blanket or rug. He carried a haversack containing his fish lines, a box (or book) of flies, a brandy flask, matches, slippers, extra shirt, probably a tooth brush and comb and sometimes a hairbrush. To make his equipment complete he put a compass and a whistle into a pocket to be used for them alone.

It was up to the guide to provide boats if they were needed for the trip. And he must have the ability and know-how to lead his man, or men, from the home base to any desired destination and back again. He also had to be able to paddle a canoe or row a boat, and to carry either of them from one body of water to the next. A guide, and you too, needed to be capable of sitting for hours as you watched for a deer, and remain almost motionless while the black flies, mosquitoes and midgies almost ate you — and him — up.

At the evening stop, the guide would put up a "shanty" of evergreen boughs and make it fairly waterproof by covering it with bark. Of course it was up to him to build the fire, cut the wood and drag it to the fire and get supper from whatever food was on hand. Then, instead of resting after supper clean-up, one or more of the party might want to be paddled or rowed around on the lake, with a jack-light in hand, for half the night, in the hope that they might catch a glimpse of a ghostly looking deer or, at the least, hear one whistle.

Such a program pretty well filled out a day. For all this service one man alone paid $2.00 a day. If there were more than one in the party, the price was one dollar a day per man.

Strange Things Happen in Camp

"Did you ever hear about the belled black bear?" Paul might ask and so would start off a story-telling session.

"You didn't? Well, at Hunter's Home, we always have some kind of a hunt on as soon as we have everything snug and ready for the winter."

"I had heard for a long time about the hunting over in the

Sentinel Range, and one fall we went over there for a hunt."

"My foreman and two of my men made up our party. We planned to be gone about two weeks so, in order to have milk to use and drink, we took a couple of young cows along. It was a long hike and it took us a little more than two days to make it. When we finally reached the Range and found a good place to make camp we hobbled our stock and turned them out to feed."

"Everything went along fine for three or four days, and then the bell cow disappeared. We hunted for her quite a while and then gave it up supposing she must have been killed, either by panthers or bears. A little later on we found proof that that was what had happened. At the time the fact that we didn't find her bell and neck-strap didn't occur to us. Later, when we did think of it, we reminded ourselves that there were plenty of holes and crevices between the rocks where it could have dropped out of sight."

"Three mornings after the cow disappeared we were at breakfast when the feller that was doing the cooking asked, 'Did you boys hear the cow bell last night? I did!'"

"We just laughed at him, and the foreman said, 'Maybe this place is going to be haunted by a cow's ghost.'"

"But the very next night I heard the bell myself. I waked up the other boys and we all heard it. It sounded far away up on the side of the mountain. There was a queer deep tone to it, and it seemed so weird that we had some trouble laughing it off. We each had a different idea about it. The foreman thought the bell had been laying around where the cow had been killed and a deer had got the strap tangled up in his horns. The cook thought a wolf was carrying it around in his mouth. I was inclined to think a panther had somehow got it fastened onto him."

"Some of us heard it about every day, but we was busy with our hunting and so let it go until pretty near time for us to go home. Then, late one afternoon, we heard the bell right after supper. The foreman and I decided to give chase and solve the riddle if we could. 'Twas a pretty dark night and we crept along through valleys and over cliffs. We found it hard and slow traveling, but we could still hear the bell occasionally, and curiosity kept us going. By the light of morning we figured we must still be about a quarter of a mile away from the bell. We were tired and hungry, but were bound to find out if we were following bird, beast, or — *what*. So we kept on."

"Just as the sun was coming up we came in sight of a blueberry patch, and there we found our bell ringer. In the middle of that berry patch was a big black bear, and it had our cow bell hanging from the strap around its neck. How that bear had ever got the buckled bell-strap worked onto its head and up around its neck we never could figure out. But once on, I s'pose he couldn't figure out how to get it off. We hadn't thought that the bell-ringer might be a bear—and such a bear as it was—the biggest one I ever saw."

"The bear hadn't heard us, nor got wind of us, and we stole closer to him. He was trying to find enough late blueberries to make himself a breakfast. The closer we got the bigger he looked, and the cow bell was still swinging from his neck."

"The bear saw us as we stepped out into the clearing, and he stopped eating to look at us. I had looked a good many bears in the face, but I had never seen such a sad-faced one before. The little eyes that are usually beady bright were overcast with a film of grief. That look of droll good humor which is in every bear's face had changed to the look of a hunted buck deer."

"The big fellow didn't try to run away, nor charge us, but just sat down and gazed at us. And it seemed like he was looking at us gratefully as we filled him with lead from our guns. He was starving and he knew it. While that cow bell alarm was around his neck he couldn't even catch ants. Blueberries were just about all he could stalk and catch, for everything else would run away or go into hiding at the sound of the bell. But it was real late even for blueberries. They were just about gone, and even if they hadn't been, the berry patches were so far apart that he couldn't find berries enough in one patch to give him strength to get to the next one."

"So he just sat there and looked at us as though he was saying, 'Thanks for shooting me!'"

"The men back at camp heard us shooting and came out to see what sort of a critter we had been shooting at. We was hard at skinning out that bear when they got to us. Two or three of the fellows took over and finished the job, while we set and ate the sandwiches they had had the forethought to bring us. That bear's hide was so heavy it took three of us to carry it to camp."

CHAPTER III

It's Not All Easy

As Paul thought of the early days, he would realize that he must not tell only of the good, but also the bad or unpleasant things. His mind would go back to a night in the early fall of 1853. He had a party of men out on a hunting trip of several days duration. One day about mid-way of the trip they were caught in a heavy downpour. By the time a suitable spot for making camp was found they were drenched. Paul, with the help of some of the party, soon had a fairly satisfactory shelter made. In spite of the rain, a cheerful fire was soon blazing near the open side of the shelter, and a most satisfying warmth was being felt by even the coldest and wettest of the men.

When the guide opened up the canvas bag of provisions, there being no waterproof covers for pack-sacks in those days, everything the bag contained was as wet as the men. With a supply of flour and a bit of fat and salt, a guide could usually mix up a batch of "flap-jacks" that were quite comforting to the inner man. But that afternoon the flour was already soaked into a very unsatisfactory, uninteresting-looking, non-usable mess of soggy dough. So they didn't have much for comfort that night except the warmth of the fire, a cup of coffee and pipes and tobacco for those who used them.

In spite of the rain the midgies, or punkies, were out in full force and the only way a bit of relief could be had was to build a smudge, which is a fire made of a damp green material which smokes greatly while burning slowly. Those little insects, or flies, almost too small to be seen with the naked eye, will arrive from nowhere by the thousands—millions, it seems. They will go through almost anything except solid material. There bite is hot and stinging and, unless you had experienced it before, you would never imagine that anything so small could bite so big. A smudge is not pleasant to the nose, and is smarting and irritating to the eyes and throat, yet it is bearable if it keeps the savage little beasts away. And so the smudge came into use that night.

In this party of hunters was an undergraduate from Harvard. He had come to Hunter's Home with a pair of new cowhide boots, which, he thought were the very height of luxury in footwear. They had proved fine up to that day when they were put through their time of greatest trial—a good wetting. As the boots got wetter they either shrunk or the feet they covered swelled, for their owner's agony seemed to increase with every step. When the camping place was finally chosen, the Harvard man dropped to the ground and tried to remove his boots. But, even with the help of some of his companions, the boots refused to budge. He might have cut them off, but he was advised to dry them on his feet or they would shrink and stiffen so that he would never be able to get them on again. So, in spite of badly suffering feet, he was forced to wear the boots throughout the night.

In telling of this episode Paul did not say how the man slept, but sometime during that uncomfortable evening he turned to Paul and in a despairing tone said, "Say, Paul, did you ever know of *anyone* who had a decent home to stay in that would be a big enough fool to come up here and go on such a trip as this the second time?"

Looking around the group and seeing that everyone was about as comfortable as they could be under the circumstances, Paul said, "Well, I tell you, boys, it does seem as if a feller would have to be crazy or a fool to do it but 'twould astonish you if you knew how many folks there is that come into these woods every summer just to go a-hunting. And it ain't the first time for some of 'em, either. Some of 'em keep comin' back every summer, or fall, and I don't s'pose half of 'em know what they come for. And sometimes, I tell you, I don't know why they come the first time."

"We've got plenty of time, while we're tryin' to dry out a little before we sleep, for me to tell you about a feller that came up here last summer from Philadelphia. There ain't any of you fellers from down that way so you prob'ly wouldn't know him. Some of my friends sent him up here, for a joke, I reckon, and I ain't sure yet if they wanted the joke to be on him or on me. Anyhow, he was *something* to get loose in these woods.

Good Day Mr. Solomon

"This feller's name was Solomon, and he said that some friend of mine had sent him up here and that he had told him that he must be *sure* to come to my place, and, whatever else he did, he must be *sure* to get me to take him on a long huntin' trip. We-ell! I haven't found out yet just who that feller was that sent him up here, but if I ever do find out he'd better stay away from here. *Baldheaded!*"

"But that Mr. Solomon! I'd never seen anything like him before. He was just so nicey-nice in his talk and actions, and almost more lady-like than any lady you ever see. Once in awhile I'd make a mistake and call him Mr. Sillyman and 'twould have made you laugh to hear him, 'Oh! Please! Mr. Smith!' he would say, 'I pray you *please* don't pronounce my name like *that*. Why, once I had a real serious quarrel with one of the members of my own club just because he addressed me as Silly. I didn't like it at all, I assure you.'"

"Well," Paul went on with his story, "I reckon it's true what they tell you, that it takes all sorts of folks to make a world, for every little while a feller sees a new sort. But, Mr. Solomon now! I allow he beat any circus side show I ever went to! He was the daintiest, tastiest man about fixin' his self up. He had a little knife that had tiny scissors in place of one blade that he used to pare his finger nails, and he had little tweezers that he pulled out his eye-winkers with, and tooth-pickers for his teeth, and a comb and brush for his mustache and whiskers, and there was a bigger comb with a point onto one end of it to part his hair with, and—oh, all sorts of such dainty little doo-dads. And every where he went he toted all that stuff along with him; and he used all them tools every time he got dressed, or changed his clothes, and lots of other times between. You fellers ought to of seen him!"

"He come up here into this wilderness with one of them Saratogy trunks like the women use. Only his must have been the biggest he could find, for when it stood around in the way, or it had to be moved, it seemed as big as a covered wagon. And if you fellers would believe it, he flatly refused to leave any of his fixin's at the hotel, and would just take it *all* along. It had to be whole hog or nothin' with him. So, I had to tote that trunk on my back through these woods, bein' careful not to trip over the brush and stones, or bump into the trees. The trunk bein' so big and heavy I couldn't carry anything else when I had it so I had to make an extra trip for it on all the carries and walkin' parts of the trip. Then, I had to make a third trip to tote the extra canoe that had to be took

along for the trunk to travel in on that later. And when it comes
to towin' a loaded second canoe behind the one you're ridin' in
there's times you begin to find out that *all* canoe paddlin' ain't
fun. But easy or hard, fun or grief, 'twas my job to do, seein' I had
agreed to guide on a huntin' trip. But, you understand, I didn't
know beforehand quite all he was goin' to demand. Anyhow, 'twas
so we went over the carries—some long, some short—up the St.
Regis River, across the St. Regis Ponds, down the Racquette River,
and to all the places between 'em, and when we had reached the
end of what we had planned, we had to come all the way back
home again. I reckon you could figger that trunk had the most
miles of personal travelin' care any Saratogy trunk ever got."

"You wonder what he had in that trunk? Well, I'm aimin' to
tell you, for you couldn't ever guess. I didn't see 'em all at once,
but mostly one at a time when he took 'em out to use."

"The very first day out, while we was crossin' Rainbow Lake, he
had me stop paddlin' and he pulled the small canoe, that held the
trunk, up alongside him and, somehow he managed to get her
open. He dug down into it a minute, and brought up a little pink
umbrella that he opened up with a top on it about as big as my
hat. I tell you it was amazin' to see a thing like that, back in these
here woods, on a huntin' trip. He got settled down again with the
umbrella over his head, and he saw me lookin' at him out of the
corner of my eye. And maybe he could see some of what I was
thinkin', for he said, real polite-like and sort of apologizin', 'It's
really very light and easy to carry, Mr. Smith, and the sun is extremely dazzlin' to the eyes.' I didn't say anythin'. Somehow I
couldn't. And so we went along."

"Some of the other things he produced out of that trunk was
about as surprisin' to see back in this wilderness as the umbrella
was. They turned up one by one, and I always tried to be handy
by to see what was comin' next. There was a great long flannel
bag that was open at one end. He would bring that out at night
and crawl into it. Then he'd pull the puckerin' string up tight
around his neck, or under his arms, or he could tuck his head into
it if he wanted to. He said that was to keep the insects away from
him."

"But the amazingest thing was to see the way he would rig himself up in the mornin' for a day's huntin'. He would be as particular as if he was goin' to some grand ball. There was a lookin'
glass fastened into the inside of the top of that trunk cover, and he

would put the cover up, bein' careful to get the light just right, and then he'd set down on a little crossed-legged stool that he fixed steady in front of the trunk and lookin' glass. When that was all done to his satisfaction the main part of the show for the day begun. I tell you there was times I figgered it was worth all the extra totin' to see it come on."

"'Bout the first thing he opened up a case with a gold top on it, and there was some gold bottles that he used stuff out of as he went along. He would get out his razors and shave his chin; then he'd slick his mustache and whiskers with some pomade and brush 'em 'til they was all smooth and shiny. After that he'd part his hair in the middle, and rub real perfumery into it. When that was done he dug into the trunk again to bring up a boiled shirt that had a stiff, stand-up collar and wide, stiff wrist-bands. He had a pair of long leather cases with fancy little buckles on the outside edge that he pulled onto his legs. The first mornin' he put on a purple necktie, and stuck a fancy breast pin into it. Then he put on a red velvet waistcoat that had pearl buttons on it. And *then* he got out his coat. He had two of 'em with him. They each had big, shiny, metal buttons with deer's horns, and dogs heads, and guns and powder-horns and such stamped onto 'em. And there must have been as much as forty pockets in each of those coats. I tell you it was good as a circus when he wanted somethin' out of those pockets. There was so many of 'em he never could remember which one his stuff was in, and it seemed like he'd go over all of 'em two or three times before he'd happen to hit the right pocket."

"Every mornin' it would take him more than an hour to get himself all polished up and into his clothes. Then he wasn't finished for he would put a powder horn strap over one shoulder, and the strap of a telescope over the other. And he had the master of all the big knives you ever see. The blade of it looked as much as two feet long, and it had engravin's all over it. He would buckle the strap of the scabbard of that knife around his waist, so it hung down in front of one of his legs. That scabbard was all crusted over with gold emblems and such like. He never used it but once on that trip, and I've got to tell you how that was."

"I ain't said anythin' yet about Mr. Solomon havin' a gun; but he did. He had the most beautiful shootin' iron you 'bout ever see. But — Bald-Headed — he couldn't hit anythin'! Every time he'd miss somethin' he'd say it was because the boat wasn't steady. I rowed him onto as many deer as I ever did to any one man. But the sight of that umbrella, that he used constant whenever the sun was out, would scare any self-respectin' four-footed beast on earth, and it would be gone before he could get the umbrella down and the gun up. If he did manage to get his gun up quick enough he would shake so bad with the buck-fever that the deer would be gone before he got a bead drawed on it. He felt pretty bad about it because he wanted to have somethin' to brag about when he got back to Philadelphia, the same as any other feller does."

"One day we came onto a young fawn that had got lost from it's mother. I pulled the canoe up close to the bank and he got his gun up and fired. I was surprised when I see that he must have wounded it, for it set right down on its haunches and stayed there. I hadn't thought of such a thing as him hittin' it, when I'd stopped for him to shoot. But the deed was done. So I said, 'Mr. Solomon *there's* a chance for you to use that knife of yours. It's too bad you happened to hit that little feller. But seein' as you did you'd better jump out and put the poor little critter out of his misery. Hold still 'til I put you ashore!'"

"'Oh, Mr. Smith!' says he, 'What shall I do? Dear me! Do tell me what to do!' 'Why,' says I, 'there's only one thing you can do. Catch him by his ears and hold him while you cut his throat.' Well he got that scimitar of his out of the scabbard, and with it in his hand he stepped ashore. Looked about like one of them pictures you see of Columbus discovering America. The little critter was still settin' there, and Mr. Solomon went over to him and reached for an ear. But every time he would grab for an ear the fawn would dodge his head away. He looked so big, and piddlin', standin' there in all his fancy clothes in front of that little beast, with that great cleaver in hand, raised, ready for use that I couldn't help laughin', in spite of how sorry I felt for the fawn. When Solomon finally did get a good hold of an ear, and started to raise up his battle-axe for its bloody work, just as if it knew what was goin' to happen next, that little critter opened its mouth wide and gave a big 'Ba-a-a-aa' right in Mr. Solomon's face. Well, he was some surprised! And he let go of the ear, dropped the knife and jumped back all at the same time. Then he looked at me and said, 'Dear me! Mr. Smith! Oh, dear me! What a pitiful sound! I can't do it! Mr. Smith, I can't do it!' and he was almost cryin'. 'Well,' I said to him, 'Mr. Solomon, I vow you've got too tender feelin's to ever make a good hunter. You and me had better go home. Anyhow your game is gone for this time.' For while we was talking' the fawn had got onto his feet and had crippled off out of sight into the bushes. It sort of rejoiced me to see it didn't appear to be bad hurt."

"That Mr. Solomon was the softest spoken man I ever come across. Mild as a May mornin'. But for all that, he was set for havin' his own way the worst of anybody I ever took a-huntin'. Everythin' had got to be just so, or it didn't go down with him. He couldn't have anythin' any different than what he was used to havin' or he couldn't go anywhere, or do anythin'."

"But it was the trunk that was to blame for most of the trouble, and it got to where it was nip and tuck between me—that trunk and him. Couldn't tell for quite a spell which would win out—him and the trunk or me. The first big crisis we had was when we was tryin' to run the rapids in the Racquette River. The canoe with the trunk in it got away from us—well, somehow—and took off downstream ahead of us. The last we see of it was the top of that canvas covered trunk a racin' among the rocks, and whirlin' in the eddies. From where we was it looked like a bunch of ragin' tigers, chasin' each other around and about. Mr. Solomon was almost weepin' over the loss of the trunk, and all his knicks and knacks."

"Well, we caught up with the trunk after a while, as I'd thought maybe we would. It was stuck on a big rock, canoe and all, out in the middle of the river. I paddled right on by, and all the while Mr. Solomon was pleadin' with me, tearful like, to stop and see if we couldn't get that trunk. Well, before we got done we had a regular Boston town meetin' over it. Both of us was stubborn-like, I s'pose. I was bound there wasn't any use trying to take the trunk any farther, and he was bound there was. We went on by, for I was doin' the paddlin'. We landed and made camp some distance below where the trunk was, and next mornin' I went back up and brought the cargo to shore, and then on to camp. By the time that was finished I figured that Mr. Solomon and me was about finished too, or we would be when that trip was done."

"'Tain't possible for a guide to always like all the men he takes into the woods, but I was the sickest of him of anybody I ever had to deal with."

"'Twasn't right, I know, but I was so provoked at him that I declared to myself that if I had a chance I'd show him a thing or two. So one day I see a deer standin' in an open field. I called Mr. Solomon's attention to it, and I started to paddle towards shore.

He was all togged out that mornin' in full dress. He had his sword and the telescope both on, a fresh b'iled shirt with diamond studs, his pink umbrella, and all the rest of his daily outfit. Between where we was and the real shore line there was quite a stretch of water that was all covered over with a sort of carpet of floatin' moss, grass, and all sorts of green stuff, and looked just like land. I pulled the canoe up alongside of it, and says, 'There's your chance to get a fine deer, Mr. Solomon. But seein' you can't hit anythin' from a shaky boat, you can just step out onto terry-firma.'"

"He'd got his gun in hand and was watchin' the deer, and as soon as the canoe touched the bog he stepped right out. I sung out to him, 'Careful, Mr. Solomon! Look out where you're goin' to!' But he was already on his way down. There was a mountain-ous splash, and a most horrendous scream, and Mr. Solomon disappeared from view. It seemed like there was more'n four acres of that stuff shiverin' and shakin'; and mud, black as ink, was bubblin' up out of the hole. The deer was so scared that he whistled and hoisted his flag, and departed all to once. And all to once there was an awful silence. I'd just begun to worry a mite when I see a head all covered with slushy, trailin' green vines risin' up out of the hole. I reached out and got hold of his collar, and pulled him into the boat. He was the wettest, dirtiest cuss you 'bout ever see. As soon as he could breathe again, he said, 'Oh, dear me! Mr. Smith! This is *terrible*! This is *awful*! I beg you to take me home! *Please* take me home at once!' And I did."

"Well, boys, as you might guess that was the last of Mr. Solo-mon's huntin'. We went back to head-quarters, and he got ready and went back to Philadelphia." Paul knocked the ashes out of his pipe, filled and lit it, and was soon puffin' at it again. Then he went on, "Several fine fellers have been up here since then, that said it was Mr. Solomon that had told 'em about the place, and recommended it to 'em. All of 'em seemed to have got a first class certificate of my character from him. So that's all right. But me— I feel a little mite mean inside to think I got riled up enough to give him such a duckin' as he got—even though it was consider-ably more'n I'd figgered on."

"Do you suppose he'll ever come back to try it a second time?" one of the men asked.

And Paul replied, "No, I don't. I think he is one feller that will be satisfied with one trip. And I kind of hope he doesn't come again, for if he does I reckon I shall have to do a mite of public apologizin', and it isn't real easy for me to eat 'humble pie'."

Another Bog Rescue

Paul Smith had to rescue, under slightly different circumstances, at least one other sportsman from one of the Adirondack, bogs.

It was at some time during the Hunter's Home days that a gentleman came up from Baltimore for a few days of fishing. He hired Paul to guide for him, and one morning Paul took him to Mountain Pond which was not far away. There were quite a number of bogs along the edges of the pond, where the surfaces of the water were seldom disturbed. They were nice, inviting looking places, but they were anything *but* solid ground.

The guest particularly liked the looks of one of those spots, and thought the fishing would be real good there, and that was where he wanted Paul to land him. Paul tried to talk him out of the idea, but he was very persistent, and insisted on trying his luck in *just that spot*. So Paul rowed over and stopped at the chosen place. Quickly the man got out, and also *down*. For he immediately broke through the boggy surface, which lay like a beautiful green rug on the water and went down until he was waist-deep in mud and water.

Paul had about all he could do to pull him up and get him back into the boat. When that was accomplished the man stood up with arms outspread, and as the water and mud dripped off him into the boat, he shivered and shook as he thought of what might easily have happened to him.

The poor guest looked greatly discouraged, and very unhappy, as he said, "Mr. Smith, this is a very regrettable happening! I should have listened to you! I see that now. I think we had better go to the house at once." As Paul agreed with him, they immediately turned homeward.

In telling about the episode afterward Paul said, "That all happened early in the forenoon, so I put in that day's guidin' real quick and easy, for he didn't want to go out again that day."

You Gotta Keep Your Eyes Open

One summer day Paul sent two of his men to work in the garden hoeing potatoes. The garden was of good size, and it happened that the potatoes were planted on the side of the garden that was next to the cow yard.

It was a real hot July day, and the deep shade under the nearby pine trees in the cow yard looked very enticing. After a while the men yielded to temptation and went over to the fence and, leaning their back against it, stood there in the shade swapping stories. At the same time they were keeping a sharp watch toward the gate of the garden and its approach from the hotel. In case Mr. Smith should walk out that way they wanted to see him before he saw them idling the time away.

Paul did happen to be wandering about the place at just that time. He walked through the shady cow yard, and in so doing came up from behind the men. Seeing them standing idly, and noticing their watchfulness toward the house, he took pains to come up very quietly, and stood quite close behind them for awhile, listening to their anecdotes. Then in his dry quiet way he announced his presence by saying, "If you fellows should happen to get tired of standing with your hands in Paul Smith's pockets, you might try exercising those hoes for a little while."

To say that the men were surprised would be putting it mildly. They didn't lose any time in getting back to work. And Paul went off chuckling to himself at the thought of the good joke he had played on them.

A young man came up from New York City one summer, and stayed at the hotel a number of days without paying anything on his bill. Then one night he got to figuring up his board and room and all the extras he had had, and found he was short of money to pay for it all. In fact *very* short. He discovered that after saving out cash enough for his ticket back to New York, he would lack several dollars needed to pay his bill.

Quite likely had he gone to the hotel clerk and explained his predicament they would have allowed him to send the money back after he reached New York, though their policy was "cash." But as the young man thought it over, he planned that he would leave on the early stage the following morning, without making any announcement of his departure, and without paying his bill at all.

Next morning, according to his plan, he had his trunk taken down real early and loaded onto the baggage wagon. Everything seemed to working in his favor and just as the stage was ready to leave he went out and started to get on. But just then he found he *was* being watched after all, for a heavy hand on his shoulder induced him to step backward. A few minutes were passed in private conversation with Paul Smith, for the hand was his, before he was allowed to board the waiting stage, a meeker, but a wiser man.

After the stage had gone Paul turned to those standing by, and said, "He can go back to the city now if he wants to. But he won't be able to tell if it's time to be hungry or not, for I've got his watch." Then he laughed as he said, "Thought he'd find us asleep, did he?"

More Hunting Stories

Paul Smith also used to like to tell about guiding on a hunting trip during those very early days with a party of men, one of whom had brought along a young boy, apparently as a "waiting man." This boy, Warren, was probably in his early or mid-teens.

Warren had wanted, very much, to go on the hunting trip. The men all liked his droll and rollicking good humor, and they were surprised and pleased to learn that he was a fairly good cook. He also had "great muscular strength and agility" and it was felt that he would be a welcome addition to their party. All of the men got great enjoyment out of Warren's love for, and use of, big words. So they took him on their trip, which was to last for several days.

The men returned to their camp late one afternoon. The clouds were heavy and they knew the roof of their shanty leaked. So as soon as supper was over they all set to work to repair the roof using bark from a large hemlock tree. Before the job was done the storm broke and forced the men inside. The thunder and lightning and downpour of rain continued so long that they gave up their plans for night-hunting and, after a few short yarns from Paul, and a smoke, they settled down for sleep.

In spite of the repairs with the bark, the roof leaked badly and the first man awake in the morning found that he was very wet. He stepped outside to the fire which had recently been replenished and was burning merrily, and found Warren stretched out on a good-sized log beside the fire while the rain poured down upon him.

When Warren looked up and saw his damp visitor he laughed and said, "Go 'way, ole shanty! You ain't no-wheres! Here's comfort! It melts jus' as fast as it falls, and runs right off!" And then he added, "I b'lieve this 'ere roast's a'gittin' done too much on one side!" And with that he raised up and turned himself over.

Often times the midges were so thick that when they camped they would have to have a "smudge" going to keep off "dem disreputable midges," as Warren called them. "And," Paul said, "they seemed to be particularly fond of Warren."

One night during the trip several of the men had reached the camping spot and, Warren not being there at the time, decided to make themselves a cup of tea—according to their own recipe. Of course they only had one kind of tea with them, but they were very generous with the amount of "leaves" they put into the pot, after which they set it by the fire and allowed it to boil for a bit before pulling it back where it would simmer. They seemed to be pleased with the result, and when Warren reached camp they poured him a cupful and asked him to try *their* brand of tea. He did. And there must have been a strength to it that was new to him for he said, after his first sip, "Golly! Dis 'ere's intoxticating! I's inebriated!" Afterwards he would often mention that tea, and once was heard to say, "Now, gen'lemen, dere's three kinds of tea at dis Metropolitan Hotel. In de first place, dere's Bon-bon tea; den dere's black tea, and den dere's camp tea. Now, doctors, what kind of tea do you diagnosticate upon today?"

One day when they were well on their way down the Racquette River, Warren spied a number of ruffed grouse, or partridges, in a tree. He begged the men for the loan of a gun as he wanted to shoot them himself. With the gun in hand he turned to go back to his game, while the curious men followed at a little distance. Paul Smith had been rather skeptical about there being several such birds all in the same tree, and was much surprised to find that it was true. He was completely astonished to see those birds sit there quietly while Warren took slow and careful aim. The birds dropped out of the tree—one by one. When Warren had downed the last bird Paul said, "Warren, you'll never make a sportsman for you pointed your gun at each bird as much as a minute before you fired."

"Yas, suh!" Warren replied, grinning, "but I knowed we was out of grub, so I took aim at dem fellers wid de eye of despair. I wanted to make us anodder of dem inexceptionable stews." And they picked up the birds and went back to camp to make the stew.

Hunting Wildcats

One fall a party of four lawyers came to stay at Hunter's Home for a few days. They had been in the habit of going to Maine each year, but had heard many stories of the great amount of game to be found in the Adirondacks and they decided to try their luck there and see how they liked it.

Upon their arrival at Hunter's Home, they told Paul of their change of hunting grounds, and of their reason for changing. They also said they wanted to hunt for deer and to fish for trout.

With Paul as their guide, they set out with each man carrying a share of the needed supplies for a few days of camping, as well as his own guns and fishing tackle. Paul led them through the forest to Plumadore Pond, which was about eight miles away. From there on their time was spent about equally between hunting and fishing; at the end of their allotted time they had satisfied themselves as to the number and size of both deer and fish taken.

It was Saturday night when the men got back to Paul's place. Around the fire that evening each man said he was well satisfied with the trip and they all agreed that they had had an enjoyable time. But in summing it all up the most of them said they thought they liked Maine better, and the reason they gave for that was, "Because there are more lakes in Maine."

Of course Paul was in on the above discussion, and in telling about it later he said, "I told those boys that I thought there were as many lakes here as there were in Maine. One of the men, by the name of Saunders, said, 'I've got a few more days I can spare and I'd like to see some of those lakes if you will take me to them.' So he stayed on."

Paul had a good, light, birch bark canoe, and after the other men had gone, he turned to Saunders and said, "Now, if you want to see some more water, come along. We'll get into this canoe, and I'll agree to show you as many lakes as you want to see."

Equipped with supplies for a few days of camping, and possibly for just a bit of hunting and fishing, the two men set out. They put the canoe into the water at Mud Pond, about three miles from Hunter's Home. With an occasional short carry they went on into Lake Kushaqua, across Lily Pad Pond, into Rainbow Lake, down the outlet of Rainbow Lake, on into Osgood Pond and to Follonsby Pond (which some time later was renamed Lower St. Regis Lake). From there they entered Spitfire Lake. Crossing that they entered and crossed Upper St. Regis Lake and then made a carry to Lake Clear.

The men killed a deer at Osgood Pond, presumably for needed food. As they paddled down Follonsby Pond, they passed the spot where Paul Smith's Hotel was to be erected a few years later. But at the time Paul had no thought of ever building a larger hotel than the one he already had at Hunter's Home.

By the time they reached Lake Clear, Mr. Saunders said, "Paul, I'll take it back. You certainly do have lakes enough. This is one of the finest countries in the world."

Paul replied, "We've only just begun. We can go on to the Saranac Lakes, Lower and Middle, down the Racquette River to the Forked Lakes, ..."

"No!" Mr. Saunders interrupted, "Let's go back." And back they went and that night they camped on the shore of the Upper St. Regis Lake, near where Vanderbilt later had his camp.

After they had had their supper that evening, Saunders told Paul he would like to go out night-hunting for a deer. Paul, of course, was willing, and anyhow his job as a guide was to keep his party entertained and contented. He had a jack-light with him which they would need for light for the night-hunting. He rigged it onto a staff which he fastened in the front end of the canoe, and then they slipped down the lake into Penfold's Bay.

Paul paddled quietly along, not too far from the shore to see if any deer might be feeding among the lily pads. Saunders sat with his gun in hand, and both men were watching and listening for sight or sound of deer. After some little time, they heard sounds of something swimming farther out from them in the water. It was a dark night, and they could not get their light to shine directly on the swimmer, so neither one of the men could see it very well. Paul thought it appeared to be about the size of a fawn and said so. Saunder thought so too, and said, "That is *just* what I *want*. I'd like to *catch* a *live fawn!*"

In trying to get a better look at the animal they passed it. So Paul swung the canoe around, and getting behind it again followed until they overtook it. As soon as they were close enough for him to reach it, Saunders grabbed the animal and pulled it into the canoe. And then the fun, or fight, began.

The light being raised up on the staff left the boat and nearby water in complete darkness. So Saunders could not see what he had caught and could only fight by feeling. And Paul could only imagine what was going on by the sounds that came from the further end of the canoe.

Paul said afterward, "There was the awfullest tussle in the front end of that canoe that you ever heard. I couldn't *see* it. But I could hear the animal scratching and clawing Saunders and snarling and biting. It didn't sound like any fawn to me, and it seemed like the boat would surely tip over. I had all I could do to keep it right side up."

"I yelled at Saunders, 'Let him go! Let him *go!* Throw him overboard! You'll drown us both!' "

Saunders yelled back, "No! I *won't* let him go! But he's *biting* me! He's *eating me up! Pull for the shore! Pull for the shore!*"

Paul did pull for the shore with all his might, while Saunders hung onto the creature and tried his best to choke it into submission. The second the boat touched shore Paul jumped out and waded to the front of the canoe to see what he could do to help in the struggle that was still going on there.

Saunders shouted, "Take my knife and stick him!"

Paul managed to get the knife out of Saunder's belt, and tried to cut the "fawn's" throat, but the knife wouldn't cut. Saunders was yelling, "What is it? What *is it? Hurry! Be quick! I can't hold it much longer!*" Paul ran his thumb over the knife blade to see if it was as dull as it seemed to be, and he discovered that the knife was still in its scabbard. He quickly pulled that off and flung it from him, then cut the throat of the still-fighting animal. When they got it into the light they found it to be no fawn that they had caught. It was a big, long, wiry, black, wildcat. He had bitten Saunders terribly on his hands and arms, and had so scratched him that his clothes were torn into tatters.

Looking at himself and then at the cat, Saunders said, "Paul, I don't believe I'll try to catch any more of your Adirondack fawns."

That was certainly one experience Saunders never could forget, for he wore the scars of that night's hunt for as long as he lived. But those scars and the memory of that night's expedition, didn't detract from his admiration of the Adirondacks as a delightful place to hunt, for he came back to Paul's every fall for a number of years.

CHAPTER IV

Dream Building

It has been said that to have a friend one must show himself friendly. Paul Smith certainly "showed himself friendly," and every man he met recognized that friendliness and responded to it. Therefore, many of the guests who came to Hunter's Home became more than guests, they became friends, true friends that stood the test of the years.

Daniel Saunders never did try to catch any more Adirondack fawns. One try at that was enough to last him a lifetime, but he was one of those whose admiration for the Adirondacks and for his host and guide, Paul Smith, brought him back to Hunter's Home each fall. From the first it was a foregone conclusion that he, Daniel Saunders, noted Boston lawyer, and Paul Smith, hotel keeper, guide, woodsman with a rather scornful opinion of "book-learning," would become close friends. And that friendship grew and strengthened through the years. It was in the fall of 1858, while on a canoe trip which took them from Mud Pond by various waters into the St. Regis Lakes, that the two men sat down to eat their lunch on a high bank on the shore of the Lower St. Regis Lake.

It was a delightful Sunday afternoon in September. The lake was in the midst of a completely wild and unspoiled wilderness. A beautiful spot with the charm of God's untouched creation still upon it. The spot would have appealed to anyone who loved the wilderness as these two men did and it surely appealed to them. Saunder had visited a great many places, but none had held quite the charm for him that this one did.

They sat and gazed about them as they did every time they came to that particular spot. As they ate they discussed any number of subjects. After a while Saunders said, "Paul, this is a lovely spot! Why don't you build a larger, more comfortable hunting lodge right here?"

Paul answered, as so many others have had to answer in a similar situation: "I might, but I can't do it. I haven't got the money." Saunders made no reply to that and the talk continued along other channels.

The subject of the conversation may have changed and the hunting trip continued, but Paul didn't forget the lawyer's suggestion. The more he thought about it the better he liked the idea, but he could see no way of working it out.

Hotel Dreams

One day not too long after this, as he was visiting with another friend who was also a paying guest, Paul mentioned the above conversation. This man, Dr. Hezekiah B. Loomis of New York City, instantly approved of the idea. He and a number of the other men who were regular guests at Hunter's Home, had for a long time been wanting Paul to build a larger building that would have more of the comforts of the modern hotel of that day. The men had no complaints for themselves about the lack of privacy, or the lack of luxury of the present "Home" for hunters. But it *was* a home for *hunters* and many of them wanted to bring their wives along on their vacations. In order for them to do that there had to be different accommodatons than Hunter's Home afforded. Dr. Loomis was so anxious for this plan to be worked out that he urged Paul not to wait, but to go at once and buy the land he wanted, if he could get it. "And," he said, "when you get it I will loan you whatever money you need to put up a good, and comfortable building."

Paul Smith was 33 years old in August of that year, 1858. He was still unmarried, and for all his boating, hotel-keeping, and guiding, he had managed to save only $300. With that as his "nest egg" he went to Keese and Tomlinson, lumbermen of Keeseville, to see about buying 50 acres of their land. As he pointed out to them the spot he wanted, he made sure that the section he asked for contained the very spot that he and Daniel Saunders had admired so much.

The lumbering company seemed very willing to sell the land, but the price of $6.00 an acre seemed pretty high to Paul who had, just a few years before, paid so much less for his Hunter's Home property. However, he realized he would have to pay the price if he wanted the land and was just about to agree to take it when Dr. Loomis, who seems to have been with Paul on his trip to Keeseville, suggested to him that he had better have the title searched first.

Paul objected to that as he felt the land was already costing more than he could afford, but the doctor insisted. The search was made, and it was found that that there were several liens on file against Keese and Tomlinson. Paul had all of these discharged in order to clear the title. From that experience Paul Smith learned a valuable lesson, and in later years he rarely failed to have the title searched before buying a piece of property.

Paul was glad to accept Dr. Loomis' offer of a loan of the money he would need for his building. And before he had finished he had borrowed $13,000. For security Paul gave the doctor a mortgage on the property and on the prospective building. That $13,000 had to do more than just put up a building, for there was land to clear of brush and trees and rocks, logs to saw into lumber, roads to make, and when all else was done there would be furniture to buy.

In looking over the place he had bought, Paul discovered there was a small log shanty on the land not far from where he planned to build his hotel. He took a close look at it and decided it would need only a small amount of repair to make a fairly comfortable place to live in while he was building. He also found two springs of good, sparkling water near the cabin, which would give them a good supply of water without too much work.

As one can see, Paul Smith was not idle during the time it took to have the land title searched. He was "spying out the land" and making plans for starting the work as soon as the land was his own. While all that was going on, Paul's parents, Phelps and Marilla Smith, and his brother, Lewis, attended to the running of Hunter's Home. And they continued to live there and operate the Home for a number of years after Paul had opened the new hotel.

When the property was finally his the work started with a rush. First was the cutting of trees and brush, the leveling of ground and the digging of a cellar. By the time the foundation for the building was laid, winter was close at hand. But this man of the woods had no intention of being stopped in his work just because of the changing season, however cold and stormy it might become. The days passed rapidly; the cold did come as did snow and wintry wind. By January of that year of 1859 the snow was between five and six feet deep and the cold was intense. But for all that, Paul was determined that the work must go on.

He and the two woodsmen whom he hired to work with him had fixed up the little shanty snugly enough to keep both the wind and the snow on the outside. Bunks for each of them, a stove, table, and a bench or two were about all they needed otherwise. And so the shanty became their headquarters for the winter.

Because the location of the new hotel was way off the beaten track all their supplies of food, blankets, dishes and clothing, as well as their tools such as saws, wedges and such were transported to the camp on the men's backs in the familiar pack baskets which were in such common use in those days. Moving into camp was not a hardship for the men, but just a routine procedure for the time and the place.

The work began at once with the cutting of the gigantic first-growth trees—pines, hemlocks, spruce, balsams and cedars. Some of these were sawed into boards at a mill some distance down the river. Some were hand-hewn into beams and joists; still others, cedars usually, were cut into the proper length and were then hand-split into shingles. (The splitting of shingles was usually spoken of as "riving" shingles.) A cleaver-like tool having a wedge-shaped blade with a handle set at a right angle to it was used for the riving. That tool was called a frow.

There were no roads and Paul had to have one, so he had to plan, clear and level his own. He did this that winter and spring of 1858-1859. To make the road as quickly and as good as possible, he connected it, at the nearest point, with an old abandoned military road which crossed the St. Regis on its way from the shore of Lake Champlain to the St. Lawrence River.

You may be sure that Paul Smith worked hard that winter for he had two goals in view. First, he wanted very much to get his hotel built and ready for the use of his friends who were so much interested in his building, and who were eagerly waiting to come with their wives and families for a portion of the summer.

His second goal was so closely tied in with the first that they really could not be considered separately, for in building the hotel he was also building a home for himself and the girl he hoped soon to make his wife.

Home Dreams

It was during the days at Hunter's Home that Paul Smith met Miss Lydia Helen Martin at a community dance. Almost immediately they were attracted to each other. Paul, the tall, big-boned, broad-shouldered, powerfully-built woodsman, with a rather open contempt for all "book-learning" and, Lydia, born and raised a true daughter of the North Country, but also a graduate of Miss Willard's Seminary in Troy, New York.

Paul and Lydia were both good dancers, and it wasn't long until she had taught him how to waltz. At that time the waltz was a fairly new dance, and had been seen very little, at least in the Northern Woods. Therefore, when these two young people waltzed together, it gave pleasure not only to them, but also to all the assembled guests who watched them.

From that night on Paul was said to be "courting Lydia." They were sure to be companions at as many of the neighborhood parties as they could get to. Paul soon became a regular caller at Lydia's home for he was determined to win Lydia Martin if possible. She was the only girl he had ever seen who interested him.

When Paul first came to the Adirondacks, Franklin Falls, in the town of Franklin, was a busy little settlement on the banks of the Saranac River. One afternoon in May of 1852, the year that Paul bought his first property near Loon Lake and started building his first Hunter's Home, a forest fire reached out and consumed the whole hamlet of Franklin Falls, destroying more than 50 buildings, leaving only one small out-building that it missed somehow. Not a thing was saved, except the people. It was all gone in one short afternoon. The cleaning up and rebuilding started the next morning—just as soon as the ashes were cool enough for clearing away. The hotel was built first and as fast as one building was finished another was started until the whole community, hotel, saw mill, school house, general store, homes, barns, etc. was rebuilt.

It was in that hotel that Lydia Helen Martin lived with her parents for a number of years. And it was there in her hotel that she and Apollos Austin Smith were eventually married.

You can see why Paul was so very eager to push forward the building of the hotel and why six days of every week were filled to the brim with hard work. But the seventh day was the Sabbath Day, the day of rest and Paul did rest from his work, and he used the time to call on his chosen lady. Although Lydia lived nearly 20 miles away from the site of the new hotel, and though Paul had no way to go but to walk, whatever the weather, Paul called on her every Sunday. There were several times the trip was made harder for him when the great depth of snow made it necessary for him to wear snow shoes.

The story had been told that there was a time in either the winter of 1857 or 1858 that Lydia Martin and her sister, Lib Martin, were spending some time at the Ferguson House in Malone, where apparently they worked for awhile. According to the story, Paul and a friend of his by the name of Bill Duane were said to be "courting" the two girls. So far as is known Paul had no horses and quite likely had hired a "rig" for the journey, and the vehicle is spoken of as being a "jumper" (which is described in the first chapter of this book). It seems more likely that it would have been a "pung," a lighter sleigh, more the size of a cutter, with a boxlike body, and a seat across the body. The pung would undoubtedly also have been home made. Duane is spoken of as "having money" and his conveyance that day was a shiny new Isham cutter.

A man by the name of Sandy Flannigan was running the hotel and he had a billy goat that had the run of the premises. While the boys were in the house "courting" the girls, Bill and Lib in the parlor, and Paul and Lydia in the kitchen, the goat was wandering around outside. In his travels about the dooryard he met what appeared to be another goat and he immediately started to butt it off the place. As often as he dove at the goat the other goat dove at him, and they met head on time and time again. Neither one seemed to be getting any advantage over the other, for Billy was fighting his own reflection, which, in the beginning had shone so clearly in the shiny mirror-like finish of the back of the cutter. By the time the goat quit the battle, Bill's new cutter was pretty well battered up. Later on as Duane looked at the damage done and mourned over it, Paul said, "Look there! He never touched my old jumper at all."

Getting Ready for Change

During the winter of 1858 or early spring of 1859, Paul made business trips to both Boston and New York to purchase furniture and other furnishings for the hotel. When finished, the new hotel contained 17 bedrooms, a large sitting room, or parlor, dining room, kitchen, etc. To many it seemed to be much too large a building for the place and the times.

Paul worked almost around the clock all that spring for he had set June 1st as the date for opening the new hotel.

To Paul, and to the people of the Adirondack wilderness, the new hotel may have seemed large and luxurious, but it could not be considered a beautiful building either inside or out. But to stand at the house and look out across the lake, one could not fail to be impressed with the surrounding natural beauty. On the opposite side of the lake were the St. Regis Mountains. Often in the early dawn they seemed to be tinted with purple. When partially shrouded with an early morning mist, fog, or low-lying clouds, they were a picture that was well worth painting. A big ragged old pine stood in front of the hotel near the edge of the lake. It leaned out over the water as though trying to see itself in the mirroring surface below. A little way out in the lake was a scraggly-looking rocky island. The occasional sight of a few ducks floating on the water, the flash of a trout leaping in the sun or the sound of a loon or two, calling and laughing in the twilight, added much to the wild and natural beauty of the place.

The hotel may have been lacking, as it certainly was, in beauty of outline and in many of the luxuries to which the city-bred were accustomed, but nevertheless there was a charm and home-likeness about it that appealed to a great many of the refined and wealthy people of the land. During the years to come a goodly number of those people would not allow a year to pass without a visit to Paul's.

In spite of long days of hard work and of correspondingly short nights for rest; in spite of times of extreme cold and deep snow, and of many miles to travel, Paul Smith did his courting well and successfully, for he, Apollos Austin Smith and Lydia Helen Martin were married on May 5th, 1859.

Lydia Martin was born August 29th, 1834 in Ausable Forks, New York. She was one of a family of eleven children whose parents were Hugh and Sarah (Goodell) Martin. For a number of years the Martins were the proprietors of the Franklin Falls Hotel in the town of Franklin, New York, and it was there that the Martin-Smith wedding took place.

What A Pair!

On May 15th the Smiths arrived at their new home in the new Hotel, and they had guests there on the 16th. One can suppose without too much imagination, that the next two weeks both Paul and Lydia were more than busy with all the last minute things that would be required to fit up a new and empty place for comfortable occupancy. However, it was theirs to work at together.

What enjoyment it must have been! While Paul and Lydia were working at that, his parents were getting the Hunter's Home place ready, for they did considerable business there for the next few years.

Even in the early days of Paul Smith's life in the Adirondacks, people who dealt with him considered him shrewd and wise in judgment; he certainly showed those qualities when he chose a wife and it does seem that Paul and Lydia's marriage must have been "made in heaven." Each of them, so different in so many ways, complemented the other to make an ideal whole.

Lydia was not only well educated, but she, too, had a strong vein of shrewdness and common sense. She must have been able to see and judge the inside of a person; why else would a woman of her education and abilities have been drawn to a man who seemed to care little for "book learning" as he called it, and for the so-called finer things of life. However, Paul came into greater contact with those "finer ways of life" through his closeness to Lydia, and his contact with his guests. Many of them were of that select group regarded as the best people of the land. Many of Paul's rough corners gradually smoothed down, and he himself took on some of those finer, gentler ways.

In spite of the fact that Paul Smith's formal education was supposedly not very great, and in spite of the fact that he had a great disdain and real contempt for "book learning" as such, there was never a time in all his years that he ever was beaten in any business deal. He loved to have occasion to use the phrase "No fool like an educated fool." With twinkling eyes, and lips twitching to speak, he loved to get the best in any argument, business deal or joke, and usually did. Paul liked to think that he didn't need education because he had been "born smart."

Lydia's education did not hurt her ability as a cook and house-keeper for she excelled at both vocations. She was a better penman than Paul, and they hadn't been married long before she took over keeping the books, making out the bills and in fact did just about all the writing for the hotel. She also wrote nearly all the contracts for her husband's business which, with the building of the new hotel, seemed to grow and expand rapidly. Upon hearing her congratulated for her ability in that line Paul would answer, "I've never lost one cent on any contracts she has ever written."

Lydia also took over the cooking as well as the book work, and from the very first, Paul Smith's hotel was famous for its good meals, even as his Hunter's Home had been. Those meals had as much to do with the popularity of the place as did Paul's personality and friendliness.

As more of her time was taken up with the paper work and all the various duties involved in serving as housekeeper of the establishment, Lydia had to give over most of the actual cooking to others, but she made sure that the same type of good meals were turned out by those who took her place. Her homemaking was such that the hotel seemed to many like a "home away from home."

Lydia Smith had a charming dignity and a kindliness of manner toward everyone. This gave her influence and great power. She also was a very generous person and her charitable deeds were always done kindly and considerately.

During the long winter months, when the "wolf might be howling" at some poor neighbor's door, Lydia always seemed to have a way of finding it out; she would send food, or clothing, or whatever was required to meet the need. Sometimes she, herself, went for miles to help out in sickness or trouble.

A Home and Children

A little less than two years after their marriage, Paul and Lydia's first son was born on March 4, 1861. They named him Henry B. Loomis Smith after Dr. H. B. Loomis who had so kindly loaned Paul the money to buy the first St. Regis property and build and furnish the new hotel. Lydia lavished much care and love upon Henry which was only natural, and especially so with a first child. But it was not many months until she realized that that loving care was going to have to reach out still further to include a new little life, for on June 4th, 1862 a second son was born into the Smith family and he was given the name of Phelps, after Paul's father.

On August 3rd, 1871 a third son was born to Lydia and Paul. He was given his father's name of Apollos Austin, and even as his father, he soon became "Paul," and was usually called and spoken of as "Paul, Jr." except by his father whose favorite name for this son was either "Paulie" or "Little Paul." With this new son, the family was now complete.

Lydia must have been really busy after that for she still wanted to carry on her work as housekeeper and general supervisor of the hotel and to help Paul. In the rooms set aside for their family use she felt her main vocation in life was to create a happy and secure home life for her three boys, her husband and herself. Because she desired to bring her sons up in godly ways, a family altar was established in that home, at which the whole family gathered daily. Lydia tried to make it a time and place of true worship, where one could meet God and be met by Him. Any person who was fortunate enough to be invited to join in this portion of the family life came away much impressed by the sanctity of it.

At some time during those early years in the new hotel Lydia's brother, Charles Martin, began to work at the hotel as desk clerk. At about the same time, he started a school for young children, which was held in one of the hotel rooms, with the term starting in the fall as soon as possible after the last guest was gone. Supposedly the Smith boys attended their uncle's school for their first few years, and when they were older and better able to go the greater distance they may have attended the district school in Brighton.

We know that Paul Smith had a great love for the Adirondack Mountain region, and it seems that even in that respect he had found a true mate; Lydia's devotion to the mountains, and especially to her mountain home, showed a love and loyalty to match his own.

There are all kinds of people in the world and among them are persons who have regard only for money, or the things it can buy. They have comtempt for things which are not from the city, dislike anything that smacks of the country.

Just such a guest came to Paul's back in those early days of hotel keeping. *Why* he came was hard to understand. From the very first he was strutting around, doing his best to display his wealth, trying his best to prove to those around him that there were none there so rich as he. He made all sorts of sarcastic remarks about the location of the hotel, and about the rugged scenery, to anyone who happened to be standing near. This man also broadcast, to one and all, many belittling remarks concerning the way in which the hotel was run. He complained about the lack of services and conveniences that every hotel ought to have. Because of this, the man wasn't at all popular, and was left very much to himself.

He had been at the hotel several days when Mrs. Smith overheard him making some of his critical remarks. With her usual dignified bearing she stepped closer to him, and said in her quiet way, "Young man, you are evidently out of your proper sphere

here. You should either return to New York City, and stay there or else you should bring the city up here with you." She turned and walked away, and he made no reply as far as was known. But the young man felt her rebuke, and apparently profited by it, for he was heard to make no more such remarks during his stay.

Mrs. Paul Smith always seemed to be a little more reserved than her husband was, but she was just as friendly. She was just as proud of Paul as he was of her. She was very plain and neat in her ways, put on no airs, and managed the home-making part of the hotel business as well as he did the outside. Mrs. Smith always had pleasant relations with the help. She liked to hear and tell little stories and anecdotes and she had one simple little tale that she seemed especially to enjoy telling about Paul.

She would say: "One fall a guide went to Paul and said, 'Say, Paul, can I keep what I just found back there?' And Paul answered, 'Yes, if it ain't worth more than ten dollars.'" Then Mrs. Smith smiled happily, and added, "That was just like Paul. And when the guide showed him a silver cup he had found, Paul looked it over, and as he handed it back he said, 'I guess that ain't worth more than ten dollars, of course you can keep it.'"

CHAPTER V

Hotel Success

From the very first Paul's hotel was a success. It bore only the name, "Paul Smith's," and was known far and wide as a house of excellent entertainment and such it was. The entertainment was simple and primitive to be sure, for it consisted mainly in allowing guests to do just about as they pleased. The enjoyment of the tasty meals that Lydia cooked, and Paul's ability to tell a good story added up to great entertainment. It was not many years until it became one of the best known, and best loved summer resorts in the United States.

It soon became a fad with the rich and the great of the land to go to Paul's, and the same people were to be found there year after year. Yet, Paul never "toadied" to the rich or gave them more honor or service because they had larger bank accounts than some other men. A penniless man got just as much attention from him as the millionaire did. Perhpas that was what appealed to the millionaire, the fact that he was accepted at face value, rather than at pocketbook value. Certainly it wasn't because they were coddled and catered to excessively. Luxuries such as bellboys and porters, and modern bathrooms were slow in being added to the hotel.

Help Yourself

One day during those early days of Paul's hotel a brand new guest arrived. He had apparently never heard anything about the policies of the place, of its luxuries, or its lack of them. Soon after being assigned to a room he began to ring what he supposed to be a service bell. By the end of a half-hour of ringing and waiting, and then ringing again he was tired of it, and thoroughly angry at the whole establishment for their lack of service. So he went downstairs to complain at headquarters. Of course "headquarters" was Paul, and the guest searched until he found him in his favorite spot on the front piazza.

Paul was not only in his favorite spot, but he was busy at his favorite occupation, the telling of one of his favorite stories to an appreciative audience. He sat with his chair tipped back against the house wall, and with one hand raised he was building up to the climax of his story. Just then his very angry guest came in view and stepped close in front of Paul, who never liked to be interrupted at such a time. He dropped his hand, and concealing his annoyance, asked quietly, "What was it you wanted?"

The guest replied angrily, "I want some water."

Paul let his chair down onto its legs, stood up, and went inside the house. He returned almost at once with a large water pitcher which he held out to the guest. Then he pointed at something at the end of a path a little distance away from the house, and said, heartily, "There's the pump. Go and help yourself. Be sure and take all you want for we have plenty of water, enough for everybody here." And so saying Paul went back to his chair to finish his story, while the speechless guest went to the pump for the much desired water.

This may sound like there was a lack of courtesy, but no discourtesy was intended. It was the way in which the house was run. There were no bellboys to wait on the guests, hence every man, or woman, had to look after him or herself. They either liked the primitive ways or they didn't. After all it was a primitive place. Paul did nothing to influence them either way. No change was made in the usual policy to favor anyone. If the guest didn't like the way things were run, he might growl and leave in a huff if he wanted to. But very few ever did that. Most of them laughed and stayed, and apparently liked it, for they came back again and again. And they brought family or friends with them, so that they, too, could enjoy the fine hospitality there.

War Comes

The Civil War years were especially successful years for Paul Smith's hotel. One wonders why this should have been. Were the North Woods so far away from the war area that one could hide away from it completely? Or did the busy man find it a place where he could gain rest, strength and energy before going back into the fray? Whatever the reason, they came in such numbers that the time proved to be profitable to Paul. At the close of the war he had paid off the mortgage that he owed to Dr. Loomis, and had money left. With this he made some improvements on the hotel and bought some more land.

Paul Smith had come to the conclusion that Adirondack property, especially that with lakes, or lake fronts, was going to become increasingly valuable. So he began to watch for chances to buy acreage at reasonable prices.

When he first heard that the Mutual Life Insurance Co., of New York City, had foreclosed a mortgage on 13,000 acres of land that adjoined his property he thought he would like it, although he knew that the spruce and pine trees, which were considered the most valuable at that time, had been lumbered off. The trees that were left, such as the hemlock, maple, birch, beech and black cherry had very little commercial value in those days. Paul hardly thought the land was worth the $20,000 that was being asked for it. He was still a bit undecided when he heard that Smith W. Weed, so-called "lumber king" of Plattsburgh, wanted the land and he decided it must be worth more than he had realized. With that in mind, he immediately slipped quietly down to New York and arrived at Col. Stone's office in the Mutual Life Insurance building so early in the morning that only a scrub woman, and an office boy were there.

Paul waited for Col. Stone to come in and immediately stated his business. He "laid all his cards on the table" at once and told the Colonel that he wanted to buy the Adirondack land his company had acquired, that he would make a down payment of $1,000 in cash, $9,000 more on taking possession of it in 60 days, and give them a mortgage on it for the remainder of the price. The company's lawyer agreed to this and dictated a contract to that effect. While his secretary was typing the paper, a telegram came from Mr. Weed informing the Insurance Company that he wanted to buy the land, and that he would pay them their asking price of $20,000 in cash.

Paul heard the telegram when it was delivered and felt that they would surely want to back out of their bargain with him, seeing no papers were signed and no money had passed hands. He said afterward, "I felt my heart drop clear into my boots. I didn't say anything, but I made up my mind that I was going to have my contract signed, or Col. Stone and I would come to blows." Paul worried needlessly for the Colonel didn't hesitate an instant in the preparation of the contract that he and Paul had just made. And that contract was very quickly finished, signed, and turned over to a very happy buyer.

A few days later Mr. Weed came up from Plattsburgh and offered Paul $5,000 for his day's work, which in reality would be giving back the thousand dollars Paul had paid on the land, and he would be paying the $4,000 for the contract. Paul refused the offer. Mr. Weed then offered $10,000, but Paul again refused saying, "No, I want the land."

There were probably some who thought Paul was foolish not to have sold it, but not very long after he had finished paying for the property and had received the deed, he sold five acres to the Garretts of Baltimore for $20,000. He thus had the full price of the property back, minus the interest he had paid. And he still had 12,995 acres of the land left.

For most people such an amount of land would be enough, but for Paul Smith it was only a good beginning. He continued to buy large tracts of land cheaply, and then sell smaller pieces at higher prices. He was generally foresighted and shrewd, and only once, when he was feeling "land poor" did he fail to take advantage of a good opportunity. He had a chance to buy 40,000 acres of valuable land for $1.50 an acre and passed it up. This tract of land was later bought by the late William G. Rockefeller. It was the only good bargain in land that Paul ever missed. He continued to buy land, some of it from Keese and Tomlinson of Keeseville as his first tract had been, at $1.50 an acre, until he owned between 30,000 and 40,000 acres. This acreage included ten lakes, or ponds, which were completely on his land.

Working Together

Although Paul Smith had many of the country's most noted and richest men as his guests for various lengths of time, and could call many of them "friend," he never reached the time when he would "look down upon" even the poorest or the most ignorant person. Instead he would always help and encourage, if he could.

One summer he hired a French boy to help with the outside work which had gotten behind. He came from the Upper Kilns (otherwise known as the French Settlement) approximately halfway between Franklin Falls and Black Brook. To come to a place like Paul Smith's was a completely new experience for the youth, and no one would know that better than Paul. He seemed rather lost and bewildered, but he was a strong, up-standing, good-looking lad, who spoke English, though very poorly, and gave his name as "John."

The first morning after his arrival Paul handed him a double-bitted axe, knowing full well that John had been brought up with one in his hand. Then, instead of sending one of the men, Paul himself went with John to show him what he wanted him to do.

As they passed the laundry some of the girls who worked there stopped working long enough to watch the two pass by. John seemed as willing to look at the girls as they were to look at him, and when they were past Paul said, "How do you like the looks of my girls, John?"

It seems that one of them had especially taken John's eye, and he replied, "She pretty good lookin' girl, dat."

During the winter a few trees and some smaller brush had fallen across the various footpaths that led to the garden and to Lake Osgood and other lakes, and Paul set John to clearing the paths.

John took a bite from his plug of tobacco and started chewing as he started chopping. Some good-sized trees had fallen because of the weight of the snow, or the strength of the winds, so it was no child's task that he had been given to do. But John set to work with a will and the chips flew high and wide. As he got a tree trimmed and a log chopped off Paul would help him roll it out of the way. Once when they were trying to move a large and heavy hemlock log that was a little stubborn about stirring, Paul said, "Well, John, that log seems to be heavier than a dead minister." That saying, "heavier than a dead minister," was one that John had never heard before and it struck him as being very funny.

At noon the boss and his hired man went to the hotel for their dinner; then back to the woods again for the afternoon's work. Paul stayed with John all that day to help and encourage him, and to help him get over his first feeling of strangeness in the new environment. By quitting time late that afternoon they had completely cleared the path that led from the hotel to the shore of Lake Osgood.

Paul stood and gazed out across the water as they were about to start home, and he noticed a few water lilies fairly close to the shore. Turning to his companion he said, "John, if I were you, I'd walk out on that old stub there," and he pointed to an old pine tree that had fallen over, with one end in the water, "and I'd pick those two water lily buds that look close enough for you to reach. Then I'd take 'em along to the house, and I'd give 'em to that girl we saw in the laundry this mornin'. That ought to make a big hit with her. I wouldn't be surprised if she likes you some already, for she asked me this noon what your name is. And I told her you owned a log house in Upper Kiln."

John liked Paul's suggestion, and started to walk out on the old tree. Then he heard Paul say, "Look out now! Be careful you don't fall in, or you'll get your tobacco wet."

That saying also struck John as an amusing one, and it set him to laughing. But he didn't let his laughter disturb his balance on the old log, and he was soon back on solid ground with the two lily buds in his hand.

They went along to the house in pleasant companionship, but John was unable to find the girl. However, that disappointment didn't dampen his spirits too much, for he was filled with enthusiasm about his new job, and especially his new boss.

Later on when he ran across Ed Noyes, and found him in a listening mood, he said, "That Mr. Smit', he nice man! He no stuck up bit. He take me out in woods to chop out path. He smoke good seegars, and help John roll log out path. By-n-by he say, 'Let me take axe. I chop tree. You set 'while an' rest.'"

"When we roll big log he say, 'Log heavy like dead min'ster.' And when we git big pon' Osgood he say, 'John, I you, I run on log, pick pon' lily, take home, give good lookin' hired girl; only look out, no fall off log, get toback wet.'"

"Then we go home. He say, 'Good man, John, wid axe. Chop good today.' Then he give me one dem beeg seegar. Funny man, dat! He dam nice man, dam!"

A Good Story Breaks the Ice

Paul believed that wit and shrewdness were inborn, or else a person didn't have such qualities; a person having such qualities learned and profited by the experiences that came to him in life. It would seem that Paul was almost proof of these beliefs for he was surely born with natural wit, keenness of thought and insight. In spite of his meager schooling he was able to "hold his own" with all those of higher education who crossed his path.

Paul loved people and was always surrounded by them. He believed there was a little bit of "humbug" in everyone, and he liked to search it out and bring it to light. This he did in a spirit of fun, trying to make his victim appear comic or ridiculous. But he was never critical or mean. To joke with one was Paul's way of getting acquainted. And when he laughed, everybody laughed with him. Paul always enjoyed jokes and used to love to tell about the results of them afterward. Of one such he said:

"I reckon the funniest thin' that happened here this summer was when two Englishmen came to the hotel. They each had a title, and they each wore a monocle and spats. They really looked like dudes."

"A lot of us were settin' around the fireplace and we got to talkin' about the best way of catchin' fish, lake trout in particular. The two Englishmen were in the group and they seemed to be specially interested in the talk, and they appeared to be takin' it all in, as we all hoped they would. Then somebody mentioned, for the Britishers' benefit, that the best luck he ever had catchin' lake trout was when he used snuff for bait."

"'Eh! What?' said one of the men. And the other one straightened up and said, 'Most extra-awdinary, upon my word!'"

"'It's a fact,' the first feller said. 'By the judicious use of that pungent preparation of tobacco called snuff, you can go out most any night and get all the fish you want. You can do it without very much effort, too. And, you know, it's a funny thing but I've never heard of anybody using this sort of bait but myself.'"

"'But, I say!' one of the Englishmen demanded, 'How in the bloomin' blazes can you catch fish with snuff?'"

"'It's perfectly easy,' the feller that was pretending to be an expert said. 'Of course you have to go out when everything is real quiet, say just after nightfall, and find a place where the fish broach, where the bubbles come out as they make that grunting sound, you know.'"

"This man stopped talkin' for a minute and the Englishmen moved their chairs up a little closer. 'Then,' he went on, 'you sprinkle your snuff carefully about on the water, taking care not to spread it too thin in any one spot. After that you have to wait a bit. But be sure and be ready for what happens next. When that snuff gets down to the fish, and gets into their nostrils, you can imagine what happens. The fish just *have* to sneeze. Now, you know, the pressure of the water is so great that sneezing below the surface is real difficult, and not likely to be very satisfying. The result is that the fish immediately rise to the surface. They poke their noses into the air, give a big '*kerchoo-o-o!*' and then down they go again. But in just a minute back they come for another 'ker-choo.'"

"'Now *this* is what you've been waiting for and have to be

prepared for. You must be sure to take with you a light, short stick with a weight on one end. A golf stick works good for that. You hold the stick in the right hand, and in the left hand you have a short-handled dip net. The second a fish shows his head above the water (of course if there's more than one at a time you try to pick out the biggest), you give him a light tap on the top of his head with the weight on the stick. You hit him just hard enough to stun him a little, and this causes him to float. Then the rest just depends on how handy you are at using the net.'"

"You'd a laughed," said Paul, "to see how those Britishers drank it all in. But they didn't ask any more questions, and pretty soon the party broke up."

"That evening when I went down to the store the man in charge said, 'Say, Paul, what have those two Johnnies that are staying at the house got in mind? They came in here just before supper and bought a whole pound of snuff.' I didn't make him any answer, but I couldn't help chucklin' to myself a little."

"Nobody saw any more of the two Britishers that evening. But the next mornin' the bunch of fellers that were in on the joke were very much on hand when the two men came back from their fishin' trip just about in time for breakfast. They were both tired out and looked it. They had spent the whole night sittin' in a row boat, casting snuff on the water while they watched and waited, club and dip net in hand, for the fish to come up and sneeze. There was nothing said by any of the men as they came together at the house except a few 'Good mornin' greetings. But the two fishermen must have caught on that they were the butt of a joke, for they looked pretty sore."

"The story leaked out around the hotel, but not by the Englishmen telling it. Everywhere they went people would sniff and snicker, blow their noses or sneeze. Some of it might have been accidental, but the two fishermen wa'n't in any mood to think so. And after a few days they got tired of it and packed up their goods and got ready to leave."

"At his last meal here, which was breakfast, one of the men had an adventure that made him pretty mad."

"I was sitting in the lobby visiting with one of the Britons when the other came out of the dining room; he was looking real disgruntled."

"The feller I was talking with looked up, and said, 'What's the matter, old top?'"

"'It's the beastly waiter!' he replied."

"'What did he do? Give you a burnt chop?' my companion said."

"'No! No such thing. But fancy! I asked for a bit of sheepshead, which was there on the breakfast card, as plain as day. What do you think the blitherin' idiot did? Why, he brought me a fish! *That's* what!'"

"And that," said Paul with a chuckle "is just about the funniest thing that happened around here this summer, so far as I can remember now."

"The two men went off to their rooms to get their traps. And then to the office to pay their bills. After awhile I come by where they sat a-waiting for the stage, and I see the one poor feller was still mad about his breakfast. At first I thought it didn't matter. Then I realized it wasn't very good policy to have our guests go home mad. So I stopped and tried to explain that the waiter had done no wrong that morning. That the sheepshead he had ordered wasn't mutton, or lamb, as he seemed to think it would be. But it really was the name of a variety of fish that are sometimes caught in Lake Champlain. And that we had a chance to get hold of some of 'em occasionally, and when we did we served 'em to our guests. It took some explaining, but I guess he finally let it sink it. Anyhow he looked a whole lot happier when they boarded the stage for the Forks."

Side Hill Creepers

Paul used to enjoy entertaining a certain type of guest with a story about "side hill creepers."

(The caution about "side hill creepers" was given by many of the "old-timers" to anyone whom they considered to be green enough to the ways of the backwoods to "bite.")

At least once Paul misjudged his guest's gullibility, and he always enjoyed telling about it.

"One time," he would say, "a feller came to the hotel for a week of huntin'. He was a young Englishman, and he decided he wanted to do his huntin' without the services of a guide."

"The mornin' after his arrival he started out alone, with his gun in hand. As he passed by me I said, 'Watch out for the side hill creepers.'"

"He stopped by my chair and lookin' very serious he said, 'What is a side hill creeper?'"

"I said, 'It's a real ferocious animal that lives just on side hills.

It's left legs are longer than it's right legs are, so it can only run *around* the sides of the hills. If you happen to meet one you must be sure to run either down, or up, the hill, because the way the animal is built it will keep him from catchin' you.'"

"The Englishman assured me he would remember, and he went on his way. And I didn't see him again until he got back fairly late that evening."

"I said to him, 'Well, I see you managed to dodge the creepers all right.'"

"'No! I didn't,' he said. 'I met one.'"

"'You did? How'd you get away from him?' I asked."

"He said, 'I just ran up the hill.'"

"'You hadn't ought to have done that,' I told him. 'You could have made better time if you'd run down the hill.'"

"'I knew that, of course,' the feller said, 'but I couldn't. You see I met a hook-tail bear just as I started down the hill, so I had to turn around and run up.'"

"'How's that?' I reckon I was so surprised and interested in the way he was playin' up about the side hill creepers that I didn't rightly take in what he was sayin' 'bout the bear."

"'Why you see,' he said gravely, 'when a hook-tail bear runs, he goes real fast. And the only way he can stop himself is to hook his tail around a tree. If I'd have kept on running down the hill he could have stopped himself and caught me. But when I ran up the hill, every time he was close enough to catch me, and he hooked his tail around a tree to stop, it stopped him so quick that it jerked him over backwards and he went rolling down the hill; and so I got away from him.'"

Paul would grin as he thought of how he had "bit" on that one. Then he was quite likely to add: "When that Englishman left the hotel at the end of the week I didn't charge him a cent for his keep. I figgered he earned it by getting the best of me."

Guides Are A Rare Breed

If the people of the North Country had been divided up according to the caste system, as it was in India some years ago, the Adirondack guides would have been in a class by themselves. Indeed, even as it was it seemed that it set a man on a pedestal, somewhat above the common run of workman, if it could be said of him that he was a guide. He always seemed to receive a certain amount of honor, and was granted more privileges by those for whom he worked.

One summer a guest from New York arrived at the hotel on the horse coach in the early evening. It was his very first visit to the Adirondacks, and having heard of the way of life at Paul's he seemed to think his first need was a guide.

Soon after finishing his supper he came across Paul sitting on the veranda, smoking one of his favorite cigars. The guest began to unburden his mind; "I was down to the boat house just now," he said, "in quest of a guide, as I wish to engage one. The man whom I addressed informed me that he was already engaged, but he directed me to another guide whom he thought was open to an engagement. When I stated my needs to that man he appeared very indifferent, and acted much as though he didn't wish to enter my employ. I don't see what is the trouble. I fail to understand it.

Just what was the trouble Paul didn't know, of course, but he did know that some of the guides were choosy, and if one of them happened not to like a man's appearance, or his personality, he would quite likely refuse to be hired by him. Naturally, if the guest complained to Paul, he had to give something as a possible reason for the refusal. And, of course, he could not tell the guest that the guide probably did not like his looks, or his personality. To that particular guest that evening Paul said, "Probably he thought your clothes wouldn't fit him. You know you can't often hire one of these guides unless he feels pretty sure your clothes will fit him." As that guest and the men with whom he had talked were of different sizes, the reason for the refusal satisfied him and he went out looking for a guide of his own size.

He's a Shrewd Operator

There was a certain campsight on the Lower St. Regis Lake that Paul considered especially choice. He hung onto it for quite a while, but finally decided to sell it if he could find someone to pay him $3,000, which he considered a fair price. He eventually found a man who agreed that it was a beautiful spot, and that it would be a choice location for a camp. After some time had passed he asked Paul if he would be willing to sell the campsite they had talked about, and, if so what would his price be. Paul replied that he would sell it, "But," he said, "I will have to talk with the boys" (his sons, Phelps and Paul) "about the price."

Paul soon managed to see the boys and told them that he had a prospective buyer for that certain piece of land. And he added that he thought they "might be able to get a good price for it." But he didn't tell them the price he had set in his mind.

The boys had inherited some of their father's ways and business ability; therefore, when the guest sought them out, and told them his desires, they quoted him a price of $10,000 for that particular site. The man still hadn't recovered from the shock when he met Paul, Sr. again. He burst into speech with, "Paul Smith! What do you think those boys want for that campsite?"

"Don't know," Paul replied.

"Well, they want $10,000," the guest said.

"*Too much! Too much!*" Paul fairly shouted. "They are *robbers!* Why, I'll sell that campsite to you myself for $6,000, and I'll take my chances with those boys."

And sell it he did, at twice what he had planned to ask for it.

More Shrewd Operations

Paul Smith built and stocked a store a short distance from the hotel from which could be purchased hardware, camp supplies and furnishings, food and just about anything that could be needed by the campers or the local people. He could give advice on the hiring of reliable carpenters. He also had teams and wagons that could be hired for hauling of lumber and other supplies.

The camp owners and their guests traveled from their homes, by rail, to the station nearest to Paul Smith's hotel. No matter how many miles that station might be from the hotel, the person that was arriving was more than likely to say, "I want to get off at Paul Smith's station," instead of "at Ausable Forks," or wherever. It was so designated because that was the end of the line so far as getting to his place was concerned.

From the station travelers were transported by Paul Smith's stage or coach to Paul Smith's hotel. From the hotel to their camps they traveled either by boat, or by team and wagon, which were all hired from Paul. He also hauled their baggage. While in camp almost every item they needed was bought at Paul Smith's store.

For quite a number of years the hotel and all the people of the area were served by the nearest post office which was nine miles away at Bloomingdale, and for some years the road wasn't much more than a trail. In the winter time it took so long to make the trip, a good part of the time on foot and on snowshoes, that the mail was usually sent out and picked up only once each week. This was quite an inconvenience to Paul as well as to many of his guests, even after they began to make the mail trip three times a week. Therefore, it came to pass that a post office was applied for. In the course of time the request was granted and a post office was set up in Paul's hotel. It was given the name "Paul Smiths," and Paul Smith, himself, was appointed post master for the new post office. As time passed, Paul seemed to have a permanent appointment, for he held the office continuously for more than 20 years, regardless of which political party was in power. When someone would ask him how he managed it, Paul would explain, "Well, I guess there ain't ever been a time that the administration could change its politics any quicker than I could."

CHAPTER VI

Famous Friends

Very few people ever met Paul Smith without having the desire to know him better.

Not the least among those who wished to call him friend was Dr. Edward Livingston Trudeau, who was later to become world-famous for his work among tubercular invalids.

It was in February of 1873 that Edward Trudeau's own physician gravely told him that he had "active tuberculosis." Trudeau well knew what that meant, for up to that time no cure and no real help had ever been found for "pulmonary consumption," as it was then usually called. It was considered to be just about the most fatal of all diseases.

Only those in a like situation could fully understand what such a pronouncement would mean to a young man of twenty-four. The world seemed suddenly to turn completely dark. It was only a matter of time, how much or how little, no one knew. Less than eight years before, Trudeau had cared for his own brother, had watched over him night and day as he suffered with the same dread disease for three long months before death came. The memories of those dark days crowded in. And he knew that the words his doctor had just said meant that he, too, was soon to suffer and die. He had never thought of death for himself.

Trudeau wondered how he could be ready to die? He had been working at his much-loved medical profession for about two years, and was getting a good practice built up. Thoughts came of his lovely wife of less than two years, of their small daughter of only a few months, and, of the new little life to be added to their family in late spring. How could he *ever* be ready to leave them? How could he *ever* tell his wife of this fearful verdict? They had been so happy!

The news *had* to be told. As he and his wife discussed the matter it was agreed that he would obey his physician's instructions that his life might be prolonged as much as possible. He immediately gave up his medical practice.

Edward Trudeau was already a very sick man. He faithfully did whatever his doctor suggested, but his condition only grew worse. Toward the end of April he was in bed much of the time. His doctor friends all began to urge him to go at once to the mountains. Not because they expected he would be helped, but because they knew he loved the mountains. He absolutely refused to go anywhere until after the new baby arrived and until he was sure his wife was all right.

In trying to decide what mountains he would like to go to, Trudeau remembered two short summer trips he had made with Lou Livingston and his mother to the Adirondacks. He remembered, especially, how much he had enjoyed each short stay at Paul Smith's. He thought with longing of the wilderness, the great forest, the beauty of the lakes, the surrounding mountains, the restfulness and peace and the free and quiet life at Paul Smith's. He thought also of the geniality of Paul Smith himself, with whom he had become somewhat acquainted on those trips, and he remembered how he had hoped to build that acquaintance into a real friendship. That feeling had been renewed and strengthened by an event that had occurred just a few days before.

Trudeau's friend, Lou Livingston, had come for him and together they drove down to Union Track, on Long Island, where there was to be a shooting match between Paul Smith, the noted guide and hotel-keeper from the Adirondacks, and a prominent Stock Exchange man by the name of Harry Park. The targets were to be moving birds which neither man had ever shot at. The winner was to receive 1000 potatoes. After their contest a dinner was served and a pigeon-shoot followed, which was open to all who wanted to pay the five dollar fee to enter. Lou Livingston planned to take part in that in hopes of winning some money, and suggested that Trudeau might enjoy it although he had never shot at pigeons.

There were a good many "sports" present and they had quite a hilarious time as they watched the futile efforts of Paul Smith and Park to shoot the pigeons as they flew from the trap.

Trudeau was "miserably ill" and, as there were liquid refreshments at hand, he drank a glass of champagne which revived him somewhat. And as it looked like fun, and they kept urging him to take part, he decided to try it. Although he had never taken part in such a meet before he won again and again, against all comers. Some of the men thought Lou had lied about Trudeau's inexperience, but both Paul and a Mr. Polhemus, whom the doctor had met at Paul's hotel two years before, assured them that it was no lie. And they all believed him, and got over their "soreness" when Trudeau used the money he had won to supply them with drinks during the afternoon.

So it was all those memories that caused him to choose Paul Smith's as a place of refuge. There was no thought of climate having any influence on his sickness.

Even in that year of 1873, the Adirondacks was still considered very much a wilderness, altogether too wild and rough, and the climate too severe and trying for women to find comfort there. In spite of the fact that back in the late 1850's Paul Smith's friends had urged him to build a comfortable house where they could bring their wives, not many of the wives seem to have come to stay very long. In 1873 the northern Adirondacks were still visited mainly by hunters and fishermen.

The Trudeaus' second baby, a son, was born May 18th, 1873, and just one week later Edward Trudeau and his good friend, Lou Livingston, started from their homes in New York City for Paul Smith's.

For hour after hour the horses plodded up the hills at a snail's pace. On the level or a not-too-steep downgrade the driver would urge the team into a gentle trot. The sick man stood the trip fairly well until mid-afternoon when his weariness and his high fever made the continual jolting of the wagon almost impossible to bear. It seemed to him they must already have traveled more than 50 miles, but still the road stretched out far ahead of them. The sun was just setting when they came in sight of the great pines around Paul Smith's. And what a welcome sight they were to one very sick, and very tired man!

Among the men who were standing near the hitching post when they arrived was Fred Martin, Mrs. Smith's brother. He was a big, strong man, and he and Trudeau had become good friends during the doctor's former visits to the hotel. Fred stepped out ready to greet the incoming guest with a hearty hand-shake. But the doctor could only whisper, "I am sick. Please carry me to my room."

Martin picked him up and carried him as though he were a baby, up two flights of stairs, two steps at a time, and gently lowered him to the bed in the very room he had occupied when he was there before. Martin had a pained expression on his face when he raised up, but instead of words of pity for the doctor's condition, he remarked, "Why, Doctor, you don't weigh no more than a dried lamb skin!"

Both of the men laughed at that idea. But Trudeau was so happy to have reached the place he had been longing to see again, that any thought of weightlessness couldn't bother him just then.

On all the long trip, and indeed ever since he had become aware of the nature of his disease, his mind had been filled with gloomy forebodings as to the hopelessness of his case. But it seemed there was a magic influence that surrounded him as soon as he reached Paul Smith's. The glimpse he got of the lake and the mountains, and the warmth of the friendliness that pervaded the place, seemed to work together to dispel his gloom. Sick and tired as he was, new courage suddenly came to him. For the first time since that verdict in February, Trudeau felt that he *might* recover. In spite of the fever, and his extreme weariness, he found he was hungry, and he ate a hearty supper, with real enjoyment, for the first time in many long weeks.

It was thus that Edward Livingston Trudeau again came within reach of the heartening influence of Paul Smith's friendship, a friendship, each with the other, that lasted through the years.

In his two former visits to the hotel Dr. Trudeau had won the liking of Paul Smith, and of several of the guides. To see him so very ill with this most-feared, and, up to that time, considered certain-to-be-fatal, disease of "consumption," inspired each of those who knew him and liked him to be desirous of giving him as much joy as possible in the short space of time which appeared to be left for him. And it appeared to them all that anything they did would have to be done quickly.

Fresh Air and Relaxation

Therefore, the first morning after his arrival one of the guides, Warren Flanders, fixed a "couch" of balsam boughs and blankets in one end of a row boat, and put the doctor's rifle alongside the couch. Then he went upstairs and asked Trudeau if he would like to go for a row down the river, "kind of slow," and "see what we can see."

The doctor was eager to go, and he soon lay comfortably on the soft "couch" in the stern of the boat, with his rifle handy across the gunwale. He was so thrilled with the unexpected adventure that he forgot all his misery and illness for the time being. Flanders kept a sharp lookout, and suddenly, but carefully, turned the boat sidewise. Off on the shore about 200 yards away Trudeau could see a buck and a doe feeding. With his rifle resting on the side of the boat, and without even sitting up, he shot and killed the buck. Flanders loaded the deer into the boat, and they went back to the hotel where Lou Livingston, Paul Smith, and several guides all came forward to congratulate Trudeau on his success.

The change to the open, mountain-air-living, in a place that he fully enjoyed, had a good effect on the doctor. He began to eat and sleep well, and his fever stayed down. Also, he spent many hours a day being rowed on the sparkling waters of the lake or river, while he sat, or lay and fished, or just relaxed and watched to "see what he could see."

Unconsciously, Trudeau was resting, and as he received only good reports from his family, who were with Mrs. Trudeau's father at Little Neck, Long Island, he was entirely free from worry. By the end of September he had gained fifteen pounds, and he felt so well that he rejoined his family.

Soon his fever returned and his doctor sent him to St. Paul, Minnesota, for the winter. By spring he was nearly as sick as he had been the spring before, so in early June he went back to Paul Smith's. That time he took his wife, their two children, and their two nurses with him. For some reason Trudeau did not gain as much that summer as he had the year before. And when fall came he still had much fever, and was very ill and weak.

Late that summer Dr. Alfred Loomis was hunting in the Paul Smith's area, and Dr. Trudeau asked him to examine him, which he did. And the report he gave to the sick man was most discouraging.

Edward Trudeau loved the Adirondacks, and especially that portion of them in the area of Paul Smith's, where he had spent so many delightful hours, delightful, in spite of the fact that during most of them he was distressingly ill. Upon hearing Dr. Loomis' report Trudeau begged the doctor to allow him to stay where he was during the winter that was so soon to come.

Dr. Loomis gave the desired permission feeling that Trudeau had such a short time to live that it couldn't make much difference. And surely he might as well spend that time where he would be the happiest.

Winter in the Wilderness

Dr. Trudeau was happy at the thought of staying in the woods. But the doctor's permission didn't solve all his problems by any means. Rather hesitantly he approached his wife next, and told her that he wanted to stay at Paul Smith's through the winter, and, that he wished she and the children could stay, too. She instantly accepted the challenge. If it looked like a hard thing to do, she never let her husband know that she had any fears about it. Wintering in the Adirondacks then seemed, and was, very hard for those who were used to easier ways. The nearest doctor was at Plattsburgh, a drive of more than 60 miles each way. Roads often went unbroken for long stretches of time, when the snow was several feet deep. If any of the family became ill, there would be no chance of outside help. Mail was brought, and sent, by a sleigh-stage three times a week, when possible, the nearest post office being at Bloomingdale about ten miles from Paul Smith's.

Although Trudeau had gotten his wife's approval of his plan, Paul Smith and his wife were yet to be won over to the "crazy" idea. At first they each flatly refused to consider such a scheme.

The hotel usually closed the last of October with the departure of the last hunter. Up to that fall Paul and Lydia and their three boys, Henry, Phelps and "Paulie," who that year of 1874 were 13, 12 and three years of age respectively, with a man to do the work at the barn, and a woman to help in the house, made up the entire hotel family during the winter. No "outsider" had ever yet stayed there even a part of the winter.

The doctor's scheme looked anything but sensible to the Smiths. As has been said, no one knew anything about treating tuberculosis, but nearly everyone thought that cold weather and storms were very bad for the consumptive. Also, Trudeau realized that his health was so bad that both of the Smiths feared that he would not live through the winter. But he begged so hard that finally Paul gave a half-hearted consent by saying, "If Mrs. Smith is willing to take on the extra work, then I'm willing."

Mrs. Smith and Mrs. Trudeau had grown very fond of each other during the summer, so the doctor asked his wife to see if she could persuade Lydia to let them stay. Finally, consent was given very reluctantly. The Trudeaus knew the Smiths were reluctant because the Smiths feared what the result might be to the doctor.

Before that winter began the Trudeaus *thought* they admired and loved the Smiths, but they were *sure* of it afterward. With the greater portion of the hotel closed off, and with no guests coming or going, they could, and did, live like one large congenial family. Each one came closer to each of the others, and each found fineness of character which had only been suspected before. Mrs. Smith was a dignified, well educated woman, with the highest of ideals, which she lived up to. She was an excellent wife and mother. As a hostess she could not be surpassed. And that winter she did everything possible to make the Trudeaus comfortable and happy.

As for Paul, they learned anew what a charming companion he could be. His way of taking everybody, and everything in life, as a kind of a joke, kept those around him from getting too low-spirited. Paul had the highest regard for his wife. She was the first and only love of his life. And he was a proud and affectionate father of their three sons. Although Paul rather scorned a high education, considering it as unnecessary for a person to have, especially if he were "born smart," he admired his wife's educational abilities, and made use of them.

Long Cold Winter

The Smiths and Trudeaus spent almost every evening together in the doctor's room. There was always a cheery wood fire which made the room very cozy; so the four of them continued the whist games, while Paul entertained them with his "yarns." Paul really liked to play whist, and got much pleasure by cheating a little if he thought he could without getting caught at it. Trudeau didn't catch on to what Paul was doing until suddenly one evening, at the close of the session, he realized he hadn't dealt the cards all evening.

The snow got deeper and deeper until it measured five feet deep in the woods by the end of February. The man who did the barn chores had to wear snowshoes to go back and forth between house and barn; and the guide who went once a week to Bloomingdale for the mail also needed to make use of snowshoes.

As yet there were no telephones, and with mail only once a week the two families were almost completely cut off from the rest of the world. There was one telegraph wire from the hotel to Plattsburgh, but there was no one to use it after the summer operator left in the early fall. Dr. Trudeau decided to learn the Morse alphabet; and he wrote to the telegraph operator in Plattsburgh to ask if he would be able and willing to help him learn to send and receive messages. The operator found his winter evenings long with nothing much to do, so he helped Trudeau for a half-hour each evening until the doctor became fairly efficient. Thereafter, the Smith-Trudeau family got world news from Plattsburgh every evening, which made them feel much less isolated.

That winter Edward Trudeau discovered that too much exertion made his tubercular condition worse; that after resting a number of hours his fever would go down, and his sickness be less. In that way there was born in him the idea that rest was better for a "consumptive" than the usually-prescribed exercise.

The children sometimes cried because their hands or feet were cold, but none of the family had colds as they usually did in warmer places. The doctor managed to keep his own fever down most of the time, so in spite of all the dire predictions made in regard to their staying in the Adirondacks, they all agreed that it was a happy, successful winter.

Of course the Trudeaus wanted to stay at Paul Smith's again, but Paul bought the Fouquet House at Plattsburgh that fall of 1875. Therefore, he and Mrs. Smith were going down there as soon as they closed the Adirondack place to run that hotel through the winter. They did what they could to help the Trudeaus though, for Paul set aside a team of horses that the doctor could use whenever he wanted them, and Mrs. Smith offered to loan them any furniture or other household goods they might need.

Mrs. Smith's brother, Douglas Martin, had been serving as the doctor's guide that summer, so the two men drove about house-hunting, first in Bloomingdale, then in Saranac Lake. They finally found an unfurnished house in the latter place which they could rent for $25 a month. Martin then drove back to Paul Smith's, and brought back a generous load of furniture, bedding and crockery and the Trudeaus were soon settled in for their first winter in Saranac Lake.

Again, according to Dr. Trudeau's autobiography, ". . . at that time Saranac Lake village consisted of a saw-mill, a small hotel for guides and lumbermen, a school house, and perhpas a dozen guides' houses scattered over an area of about an eighth of a mile. There was one little store kept by Milo B. Miller where flour, sugar, a few groceries, tobacco and patent medicines were sold, and where the clerk was the telegraph operator."

With that as a beginning, Dr. and Mrs. Trudeau spent forty winters in Saranac Lake, and every summer except one at Paul

Smith's. Often he was very sick when they arrived, but he never failed to gain much in health and strength so that each year he resumed his work as a physician for a while.

CHAPTER VII

Little Brown Church in the Vale

The Trudeaus had been in the habit of attending church quite regularly and missed it very much while they were at Paul Smith's. During the summer months there was often a visiting clergyman or bishop at the hotel and it had become the custom for them to hold services in the hotel parlor. Among those clergymen were the Rev. W. A. Leonard, Rev. Boyd Vincent, Dr. John Lundy, and Bishop Doane, (Episcopal).

After this had gone on for some time, a few of those most interested discussed the practicability of building a small chapel near by, where any visiting clergyman could officiate. Dr. Trudeau, himself, started to raise the funds for a small log building. Money and other gifts were freely given. Paul Smith gave the land, and also the logs. And those logs were the finest white pine logs to be had.

At first the chapel seated only 40 people, and it was not long until the congregations were too large for the church. Dr. Trudeau's cousin, J. Lawrence Aspinwall, gave his architectural services and so re-designed and enlarged the first little church into a beautiful building that would seat 150 people. It was named St. John's in the Wilderness and became known far and wide for its beauty and originality of design.

Soon after the little log chapel was finished Bishop Doane arrived to officiate at the dedication. Later in the day, a young woman from New York City related a bit of conversation she had happened to overhear following the service. In spite of the fact that much had been said by way of thanking Paul for his share in the project, during the service the Bishop appeared not to be satisfied, and was again using a great many words in an effort to thank Paul more adequately for land, logs and aid. Paul always hated to be thanked, or praised, and was wishing he could get beyond the reach of the Bishop's many gracious words, when that worthy man ended his remarks by saying: "I hope we will meet in Heaven, Mr. Smith."

With an air of relief, Paul replied: "Well, Bishop, when I get there I'll keep an eye out for you."

Religious services at Paul's in the early days were held in various places, and they were interrupted in various ways.

The Reverend J. P. Lundy, of Philadelphia, often came to Paul Smith's, and invariably he joined some hunting party on each visit.

On one such visit McDonald's Pond was the chosen place for the hunt. Some of the guides, among them Charlie Dwight and "Hank" Kent with his dogs, were sent on ahead. They took with them, as their share of the load, the camp meat, such as ham and bacon, which they hung on nails driven high up in the trees. They also carried other supplies and had the camp ready for the main party when they arrived the next day, which was Saturday.

Whenever the Reverend Dr. Lundy was in camp on Sunday it was his custom to hold divine services wherever the camp might be, and however few or many might be present. Therefore, that Sunday at the specified time, all the men were gathered together, respectfully listening as the Doctor proceeded with the service.

Charlie and Hank happened to be sitting side by side. It was just about the middle of the sermon when Charlie chanced to look out of the nearby window and saw one of Hank's dogs jump high into the air and pull a ham down off a nail. Quickly Charlie grabbed Hank's arm and pointed at the dog. Hank jumped up excitedly, shouting: *"Hey you! Hey! Drop that! Drop it! You, You, You — Yeller-bellied whiffot! Drop it! Drop it I say! Or I'll lambaste hell out of your hide!"* With almost the first word Hank had picked up a club, made for the open doorway and had taken off after the dog which was unable to travel at its usual speed because of the size and the weight of the load it was carrying.

The smooth flow of the Doctor's words stopped as the impact of the first "Hey!" reached his ears. As Hank went through the doorway the Doctor stepped over the window and peered over the rims of his reading glasses, and out over the top of his prayer book, to take in the scene outside. Hank was just about to belabor the dog which he had caught, but which still clung tenaciously to the ham and refused to give it up. Dr. Lundy excitedly dropped his prayer book and clapped his hands loudly together, and shouted, "Give it to her, Hank! *Give it to her, Hank!"*

Hank did give it to her until she let go of the ham which wasn't too much damaged, as she had had no chance to stop to eat it. Needless to say, that Sunday's church service ended right there, without even a benediction.

A Preachin' Blacksmith

It used to be said that many of Paul Smith's stories were told around the world, and it is quite likely that the following, which Paul told on himself, was one of the stories that traveled far.

"Quite a number of years ago," Paul would say, "I loaned a feller $40.00. He was a blacksmith, and he did some preaching whenever he had a chance. He was poor and I knew it, but I knew he needed the money, and I figgered if I watched my chances I'd get my pay sometime. So I loaned him the money. Years went by and he still couldn't pay me, but I'm pretty good at waiting and there came a time after several years that we had quite a bunch of real wealthy people boarding with us, and they wanted to know if there was any way they could have a Sunday church service."

"I told 'em I didn't see anything to hinder. The church was there, and the congregation. All they lacked was the preacher. Then I asked 'em how they'd like to have a blacksmith for a preacher. That sounded like something so different they thought it might be amusing, and they said they would be 'Dee-e-lighted.'" So I went around to see how the blacksmith-preacher felt about it and he was delighted, too."

"There was a good crowd at the service, and the people liked the sermon. And as everybody could see without a spy glass that he was a poor man, they passed the hat and they all chipped in real liberal. Before it got all around you could see a lot of $10 bills sticking up around in the hat."

"After it was all over I gave the preacher feller a nod and a wink that I wanted to see him in another room. He got the idea, and when we got in there I said, 'Now, you can pay me that $40.00 you owe me.'"

"'Sure thing,' he said. And he sounded real glad, for he was honest and had always calculated to pay me when he could. 'But,' he said, 'hadn't we better go off in the woods somewhere? It'll look kinda funny if anyone comes in and sees me forkin' money over to you here.'"

"I agreed to that. So he stuffed the money into his pockets and we headed for the tall timber. When we got where it seemed far enough out we set down on a fallen tree and we both went to sorting out crumpled-up bills, so he could give me my $40.00.

"I don't know what they thought was going on but some of the men had seen us heading for the woods and they had followed us, but, of course, we didn't know it. But we *did* know it as soon as they saw him pass that $40 over to me. They thought we had agreed to "split" on whatever came in the hat, and that we had gone out there to divvy up. They wa'n't a bit bashful about twitting me of it and it cost me several times what the blacksmith had owed me before they all got done smiling and talking about it."

Thirteen to One

Paul Smith never did get into the habit of regular church attendance, but he could almost always find some excuse that, to him, seemed sufficiently good enough to keep him at home. Evidently he was often invited, and one day he promised that he would go the next Sunday if Mrs. Smith went. He felt fairly certain that she was going to be unable to go else he probably would not have made the promise.

However, the promise was made. Sunday came. Mrs. Smith could go. Paul was a man of his word, so he went to church.

In telling about it later, Pabl said, "I got all mixed up in church. I got up when I ought to have been setting, and set when I ought to have got up. By and by I saw Dr. Trudeau coming down the aisle with a platter of $5 and $10 bills. I felt around in my pockets but couldn't find anything but a torn one dollar bill. I put in on the platter, and when I did Trudeau bent over and whispered to me, "Paul, that will return to you tenfold."

"I thought that was pretty good," said Paul, "but didn't pay much mind to it, for I couldn't see how it could happen. But 'twas only the next day that I was going down one of the halls in the hotel and heard men's voices in one of the rooms."

"I opened the door and went in and found three or four fellows playing poker. I told 'em I'd take a hand, and I did. I won $13. Then I went out and hunted up Trudeau."

"Dr. Trudeau," Paul said, "I heard what you said to me in church yesterday about that 10 to 1 business. But you had it all wrong—that is, the proportion. You said that dollar would return to me ten-fold. But I just won $13 for one in a poker game."

CHAPTER VIII

Middle Years

Paul Smith bought the Fouquet House in Plattsburgh in the fall of 1875 and soon after the last guests had gone from the St. Regis Hotel the Smiths closed up that establishment and moved themselves to Plattsburgh to operate the Fouquet House through the winter. Paul and Lydia returned to the St. Regis hotel in the spring, leaving Phelps in charge with a hired manager working under him. A few years later, the Smiths sold the Fouquet House.

We don't know why that purchase or move was made, but it might possibly have been to give their boys a better chance. Living in Plattsburgh brought them to city schools, and Henry, who was 14 that March, and Phelps, 13 in June, should have been ready, or nearly so, for high school. Anyhow, the Smiths spent several winters in operating the Plattsburgh hotel, and supposedly Henry and Phelps got their high school education there.

Through those years the Smiths hired competent men to take charge of the Fouquet House during the summer months. In 1885 Phelps, who was then 23, took over the year 'round management of the Plattsburgh hotel until his parents sold it a few years later.

Paul's Boys

We do not know much more about the education of Henry and Phelps Smith except that Phelps was a graduate of Eastern Business College of Poughkeepsie, New York, with "high recommendations" from his teachers.

When it came time for young Paul to go to school he attended the district school in Brighton, at least a part of the time. Later on he was for some time a student at Trinity School, which was a "very strict" military academy in Peekskill, New York. While there he seems to have taken advantage of most of the extras that came his way, for he took boxing, banjo and dancing lessons. He was a member of a telegraph club, a roller-skating club and rowed 4th place in his boating club.

If this had been an ordinary family of that day, living in the backwoods country as they did, these three boys could very well have grown to manhood with only a very meager amount of schooling. Their father still believed that one needed to be "born smart" in order to make much of a place for himself in the world. He also believed that lacking that birthright all the schooling in the world couldn't take the place of it. So it seems quite likely that Lydia was mainly responsible for the fact that the Smith sons became about the best educated young men in the area of their woodland home at that time. However it was, each one of the boys had a goodly share of his father's abilities born in him; as each one finished his formal education he returned to his mountain home, there to share in the work required for the successful operation of a popular hotel in the wilderness.

Not much has come down to us about the Smith boys, either as children, or as young men. They all inherited their father's liking for a good joke. Henry especially was fond of playing so-called "practical jokes," and he greatly enjoyed teasing his Grandmother Smith.

Paul's mother, Marilla Smith, lived to be 91 years old, and was blind for several years before her death. Oft times when Henry would find her sitting peacefully in her favorite chair, he would quietly drop to his knees, and would then crawl along with a soft pad-pad-pad making it sound as much like her dog, Barney, as possible. Then he would rub, or lean, against her knee, and she, apparently thinking it was Barney, would reach out to pat the dog on the head only to discover it was Henry's head. She would always pretend to be very much put-out at the trick, and never gave Henry the satisfaction of knowing for sure if she had been fooled or not. Both boy and grandmother got their own enjoyment out of the joke.

There was also a time during his growing-up years that Henry liked to hang around with the guides, and he tried to imitate them in their manners, speech and dress.

It disturbed Paul and Lydia that Henry and Phelps did not get along very well together. Even after they were getting on into young manhood they found so much to disagree about that it seemed they were in an almost continuous quarrel or argument. However, as they came into their mid-twenties and beyond, they gradually grew out of their argumentative ways, and just as gradually discovered the good in each other, and soon found themselves to be the best of friends. This change in their attitudes was a great relief and joy to both of their parents.

Perhaps because of his training in business college, Phelps was more business-like in his ways, and quite serious of manner. He was also very neat and careful in his own personal appearance. However, he enjoyed a good story as well as the other boys did. And when it came to playing a joke, especially if that joke was on their father, he could, and did, "gang-up" with the other two.

A Family That Laughs Together, Stays Together

One such joke concerned the heating of the hotel which it seemed was always either too hot in summer or too cold in winter.

Apparently the boys had persuaded their father to install a heating plant in the hotel, which he was sure was unnecessary. Anyhow, the plant was to be installed, and as the work went on day after day, Paul, Sr. announced long, loud and often, that he was sure such an outfit would never be able to warm that building satisfactorily, while his sons were just as sure it would.

When the heating plant was completey installed, a fire was built to try it out. All three of his sons, and especially young Paul, were bound they were going to make their father back down on his complaints. In the Adirondack wilderness region those days of the 19th century, wood, or very possibly coal, would have been the fuel used, and the boys soon had a good fire going. To help out with their scheme the boys secretly nailed down the windows in their father's bedroom. During the night the temperature in that room grew steadily warmer, and Paul, in his discomfort, tried to get some relief by opening a window. But try as he would, not one of them would budge. In examining them he soon found why they wouldn't open and it didn't take him long after that to figure out what was going on. So he decided to meet the jokesters in his own way, and he lay down to wait for the morning.

Morning came in due time and all three of the boys were on hand early, confidently expecting that their father would soon be coming down the stairs "blowing off steam" with every step to let them know what he thought about the whole thing. Imagine their surprise when Paul appeared on the stairs bundled up in his full-length coonskin overcoat, with up-turned collar, winter cap with down-turned ear laps, muffler tied snugly about his neck to hold his collar up, his heavy winter gloves on and not saying a word.

As he was still silent when he reached the foot of the stairs, one of the boys asked how he had rested. In a trembling voice Paul replied, "Never came so near freezing to death in my life. Why in time don't you boys get that damned heatin' outfit goin', if it's any good?" Then not being able to hold in any longer, he broke down with a great big laugh, and the boys all joined him. Needless to say, the new heating plant was credited as being a great success.

Problem Solving Father's Way

It was not many years after Paul Smith settled at St. Regis that he saw how advantageous a general store in that locality would be and it was not long before he opened up a store on the hotel grounds. He tried to keep on hand goods that might be desired by his guests, the nearby campers and also the families living in the area for several miles around.

In those days many people, country people especially, got their purchases charged, and many families would have gone very hungry at times if they had not been able to charge what they bought. There were often weeks, and even months at a time that they had not a cent. But whenever they had a pig, or a cow, or chickens, eggs, or cord wood, or anything that the storekeeper could resell, they could, and did, turn such things over to the merchant toward the payment of what they owed.

In the course of time Paul's sons were growing up, and they were taught to help at whatever work "came to hand." So clerking in the store was no new job to Phelps when his father put the store in his charge for a while. All went well for a time and then at the end of a day Phelps remembered selling a barrel of flour that he was supposed to have charged, but he could not remember to whom he had sold it. Looking on his books did no good for he had no record of having sold flour to *anyone* that day. He didn't know what to do, for he knew the store should never have to stand the loss of so large a sale.

Phelps finally told his father what had happened, and to his great joy Paul didn't seem at all concerned, but he said, "Why! That's easy, Phelpsie. All you need to do is to charge a barrel of flour to everyone that came in today. When they pay their bills if they didn't buy a barrel of flour they'll say so. And the one that *did* buy will pay for it and say nothing."

That idea seemed like an amazingly simple one to Phelps, so he set down the purchase of a barrel of flour on each of a number of charge accounts. In the course of time two of their customers complained of the excessive charge. While the rest, a half-dozen or so, each paid for the flour as charged.

Many Came

So far as is known, no one ever tried to keep the world from knowing that Dr. Edward Trudeau's health was much improved by his stay at Paul Smith's Hotel in the Adirondacks. Because of that there were soon others who were sick, and who had tried every climate, even as the doctor had, who also decided to see what the Adirondack Mountain air could do for them.

Many of the local hotels hated to take in the sick people, for they could become a great care. But Paul, with his big heart, would always take them in. No matter how dark, dreary and hopeless the future looked to them when they arrived, it always seemed that Paul's cheerfulness, his happy outlook, and his great zest for living immediately filled them with new hope, and new courage to go on.

It was during the late 1870s, and for some years thereafter, that people, especially men, afflicted with tuberculosis often came to Paul Smith's for a time. Some of them came honestly seeking health, even as Dr. Edward Livingston Trudeau had, others came looking for something new in the way of a thrill, or excitement to help them forget that the time ahead was short. They tried to fill every minute as full as possible before the end. There were some of those people whom the hotel family would long remember. And sometimes Paul told his other guests about them.

Askin' For Trouble

"One summer," he said, "a man that was pretty bad off with consumption (tuberculosis) was stayin' there for awhile. He seemed to have a good supply of money, and he acted as though his main purpose in life was to get rid of it. You couldn't imagine why it was unless, knowin' he hadn't long to live, he wanted to get rid of the money so his family wouldn't have any reason to quarrel over it after he was gone. I don't think he acutally gave any of it away, but his guide used to tell about him amusin' himself with a lot of it when they were out on the lake. The guide said that when he was rowing him around the fellow would take a handful of change out of his pocket, and he would set there in his end of the boat, and skip the coins just like you skip flat stones, one at a time out on the water, pennies, dimes, nickels and quarters. And when he had used them all up he would start in on fifty cent pieces, and silver dollars, if he had any with him. At least that is what his guide used to tell, and you know," Paul added with a grin, "all those guides was noted for being absolutely truthful. Always."

"Another thing the guides used to tell about him was that when he wanted a smoke, if there was a fire handy, instead of reaching for a splinter to light his cigar, he would pull a dollar bill out of his pocket and stick a corner of it into the fire and light the cigar with that."

"That man claimed that his doctor had told him there was a good chance of his getting well if he would stop his drinking. But he wouldn't do it. He just kept right on pouring it down."

"Prob'ly you know that a consumptive has just about as much chance of getting well if he keeps on drinking, as I would have if I tried to push old St. Regis Mountain over with my hands. He just wouldn't leave the drink alone, and almost every night he was so drunk he had to be helped to bed."

"One night he was drunk earlier than usual and had to be helped away from the table, and they took him right on up to his room, and laid him on the bed. The next morning when the chamber-maid wanted to do his room the door was locked from the inside and she couldn't get in. She reported it to the office, and a bellboy went up and went in through the transom, and found him half-way on the bed with his feet on the floor. A close look showed that he was dead."

"There was nothing to do for him then but to put him in a box, and send him out to the station on his way home to his family and friends."

Billiard Table Comfort

During the years of the latter part of the 1800s it was quite "the thing" to go to the Adirondacks for a few weeks, or for the whole summer season. At such times the more popular hotels were very much overcrowded. Some people spent the summer in going from place to place and staying one, two, or even three weeks in a place. Such guests very often talked about conditions in the hotels at which they had stayed previously. This type of guest sometimes came to Paul Smith's hotel, and Paul used to like to tell about a conversation he had with one of them. The guest was complaining about the crowded conditions at a hotel where he had recently spent the night, and he said, "The place was so crowded that I had to sleep in a room with four other men. It was either do that or sleep on a cot in the parlor where there were already eighteen or twenty other men sleeping. Not much choice, but I chose the room."

Paul said, "I told him, 'Huh! That's nothing. You'd have found it worse than that if you'd come into the Adirondacks a few years ago before there were so many hotels here. It was *really* crowded then.'"

"'Why!' I told him, 'I remember one time, back a few years ago, when a feller came to the desk to complain about his bill. The place was so crowded that we had men sleeping everywhere. My son, Phelps, and John Harding, who was here then, would have a race every night to see which one could get the last couch there was left to sleep on.'"

"When I asked the feller what the trouble was, he said, 'You are charging me too much for the accommodations I am getting.'"

"I said, 'Just where are you sleepin' and why do you think the bill is too high?'"

"He replied, 'I've been sleeping on the billiard table; that's why I think the bill is too high.'"

"'The billiard table?' I asked. And he said, 'Yes! The billiard table,' and he pulled out a bill and showed it to me."

"'*What!*' I almost shouted, as I looked at the bill; 'Your bill ain't right! It ain't high enough. We get $2.00 an hour for that billiard table. It's the only one in the Adirondacks.'"

Having finished the first story Paul was very likely to continue soberly, "But that was nothing much compared with the complaint of another feller that came up here one summer from New York."

"He'd been here about three days before I saw much of him. But that day he walked up to me and said, 'Paul, you're going to have to find me another place to sleep.'"

"I said, 'Where in thunder are you sleeping now?'"

"'Well,' he began, 'You see, it's this way. I've been sleeping on a sick man. He's been pretty sick, too sick to make a fuss, so it hasn't been too bad; but he's getting better, and he isn't going to put up with it much longer.'"

By the time the laughter had quieted down from that tale Paul might go on: "But say! You should have been around here a few years ago when there were so many people traveling into these mountains that 'twas impossible for the hotels to give 'em all a private room, or even a separate bed. Sometimes there wasn't any bed at all, but 'twas hard to make some fellers believe it when you told 'em you had no room."

Too Few Rooms

"I remember one time when every corner of the Franklin Falls Hotel was full to overflowing, from corner to corner, and from cellar to skyparlor. And then one afternoon a young feller from Boston came struttin' in, and in a swaggerin' lordly tone of voice demanded a room, 'All to myself,' he said."

"'We are very sorry,' they had to tell him, 'but we are all filled up, even to the coal bin, and the dog house. Every room we have has at least four people in it.'"

"The young swell kept insisting that he must have a room. And they kept telling him they didn't have any rooms. After awhile he said he would be willing to put up with a bed in 'any well-aired room.' When they had to refuse him again he got real abusive about it."

"Dunton was running the place then, and he felt that he knew how to run an Adirondack hotel. He always did everything possible for the comfort and convenience of his guests, but even he couldn't give accommodations where there were none. When the feller came 'round again and asked so insultingly for a 'well-aired room' Dunton decided he'd had enough. So he stepped over to the 'young swell,' and put his hand on his shoulder, and said, 'You shall have a bed in a well-aired room. Come with me.'"

"Dunton whistled for his dog, Jack, and started for the back door with the Boston chap following. When they came to the garden Dunton led the way into a good-sized bed of onions and stopped there. He took the feller by the shoulder again, and pointed down to the onion bed, and said, '*There* is a bed all to yourself, and your room is well-aired, too. *Get into it*.'"

"When the Boston feller saw he meant it he tried to be let off, but it wasn't a bit of use. He was made to stretch himself out in the bed of onions, and Jack was left on guard to see that he stayed there."

"Several times druing the night the young chap tried to get up and leave, but a threatening growl from Jack kept him in his place."

"In the morning when Dunton called the dog in, the prisoner was released. He smelled pretty strong of onions, and he seemed a much sadder, and it was hoped a little bit wiser, traveler."

"When he got back to the hotel he found the story of him and his 'room' had spread through all the house. So he didn't even wait for breakfast, but he left to hunt up another place farther up the road."

CHAPTER IX

Between Friends

Pepper Story

Nearly everywhere one goes, if he stays long enough, he is very likely, sooner or later, to hear the story about the "pepper that was half peas." No one knows who was the originator of that story, but it seems quite safe to say that it was Phineas Taylor Barnum (known world-wide as P. T. Barnum of Barnum's Circus) who brought it to the Adirondacks.

P. T. Barnum and Paul Smith were good friends for a number of years. Although Barnum was 15 years the elder, the two men were much alike in their enjoyment of a good joke and each was always trying to get the best of the other. This writer has found two different versions of the pepper story. It being impossible to discover which is the true or first story, they will both be related here, and you may each take your choice. (My own choice goes to the second version.)

One hot summer day the circus owner was spending a vacation at Paul's, as he often did, and the excitement seemed to be at a low ebb, when Paul caught a glimpse of something that looked very unusual. As he watched, he saw two men on foot coming slowly along the country road. One man was leading a bear, presumably one of the cinnamon-colored variety, as most of the "dancing bears" were, and the other man carried a hand-organ.

At least one such outfit would pass through a village most every summer. They would stop in a park, or on a hotel lawn, prop the organ up on its upright post, and start grinding out the music. Soon all within hearing were gathered around and the show was on. The bear would dance around on its hind feet, either alone, or with one of the men; or the bear and one of the men would wrestle. Always a hat, or some other receptacle, was passed by one of the men and so the show was paid for. However, it was seldom that such an outfit ever strayed so far from the beaten path as to reach Paul Smith's; hence Paul's surprise at seeing them.

Immediately Paul thought of playing a little joke on Barnum. And as the new-comers were still unseen by anyone at the hotel, Paul went out to meet them, and stopped them where the trees and brush still hid them from the building.

The men were Italians and hadn't been in this country long enough to understand English real well. But Paul finally made them understand that he wanted them to go to Mr. Barnum, and make a fuss over him, as though they recognized him and thought him the greatest ever. Paul had quite a time trying to make them understand how they could tell which man was Barnum, so he agreed to give them a signal by which he would let them know who he was. He then allowed them to continue on to the hotel.

When the men and the bear were discovered by the hotel crowd there was much excitement. Barnum happened to be sitting just inside the building near the front door, so he soon heard the unusual sounds, and stepped out onto the porch to see what was going on. As soon as he appeared Paul gave the men their cue, and bear, organ, and all, they rushed up to Barnum, and in their broken English began excitedly calling, "Oh, Mr. Barnum! The *great* Mr. Barnum! The *wonderful* Mr. Barnum!"

The crowd gathered 'round; the hand organ was set up and played; the bear danced and wrestled and the show was on. As usual at such times, the audience bought drinks for the bear — beer if it was available — which it would drink until it was intoxicated. Every little while the men would stop and make more fuss about Mr. Barnum, who, after a time became a little flattered by their attention and for some reason, made an appointment with them to meet him in the city. Just why he wanted to see them is not known, though it could be possible that he considered hiring their bear act for his circus. Anyhow, according to the story he did see them in the city, and they apparently "let the cat out of the bag" regarding the joke that had been played on him at the hotel.

Of course Barnum had to find a way to "get even" with Paul, so he wrote him a letter telling him what a splendid vacation he had just had at the hotel, and how very much he had enjoyed it. "Everything was perfect," he wrote, "except for one thing." That grocery firm in New York City that you buy your provisions from is giving you shoddy stuff, Paul. Why, you probably don't know it but the pepper you are using is half peas."

Upon reading that letter Paul was pretty much put out to think that he was being cheated like that. So he wrote to the company complaining about the pepper, and he enclosed Barnum's letter to prove that his guests were complaining to him.

The grocery company replied, and explained that Barnum was playing a joke on Paul, that he was referring to the spelling of the work *pepper*, and not to the purity of the condiment itself.

The other version of the story was told by a former clerk of the hotel. For two or three years P. T. Barnum and his wife, and their family physician, a Dr. Hubbard from somewhere in Connecticut, spent part of each summer at Paul Smith's.

It was around the summer of 1889 that Barnum said to Paul one day, "Paul, every thing about your food is first class except the pepper. And that is poor. Why, it is half peas."

Paul said, "I don't see how that can be, as we buy the very best brand that we can get." But Barnum called to the doctor and asked him what he thought about the pepper, and he agreed with Barnum.

Paul was pretty well worked up to think that a reputable firm would put out such poor stuff, so he hunted up his son, Henry, who was helping with the desk work, and he told Henry what Barnum and Hubbard had said about the pepper.

Henry was real angry about it, and he and his father agreed that there must be something done about it right away. Together they went to the clerk, and told him of their discovery about the pepper, and said, "Write to Bacon, Stickney and Co., right away, and tell them that our guests are finding fault with our pepper because it is half peas. Tell them to send us ten pounds of *pure* pepper. And tell them if it isn't *strictly* pure they needn't send any."

In a very few days there came a package by express, containing "Ten pounds of pure pepper." With it was a letter explaining that this was *pure* pepper; and it was also the same kind which the hotel always bought. Then the letter went on to say that they felt a joke was being played on Paul, that the jokester meant that the word "pepper" was half P's, and not that the pepper itself was half peas.

The clerk had just finished reading the letter when Barnum came along and asked if they had had any reply from the company about the pepper. When he found the letter had arrived he went to find Paul, and they went to the desk and read the letter together. Then, like a pair of young boys, they were filled with glee; Barnum because the joke had worked, and Paul had "bit," and gotten well fooled and, Paul, because it was a good joke he could enjoy even though it had been played on him. Boys at heart still! Though in that year of 1889 Barnum would have been 79 years of age, and Paul was 64.

To prove that he appreciated the joke, and that there were no hard feelings, Paul said to Barnum, "Call on all the wine you want." Barnum said he didn't care for any just then, but he would take some later for his friends.

While at the hotel Barnum always had a weekly bill made out for him. So he went to the clerk, and said, "Put the price of that 10 pounds of pepper, and the express charges, on my bill."

Mrs. Barnum knew nothing about the joke, and when she saw 10 pounds of pepper charged on their bill she was much astonished and asked her husband, "What in the world are you going to do with all that pepper?" And she added, "Are you getting crazy?"

It is to be supposed that the matter was explained to her satisfactorily.

Who Owns That Dog?

During those early days of Paul Smith's hotel-keeping at St. Regis Lake there was a short piece of fencing along-side the drive-way that led in, and around the corner, near the front entrance of the hotel.

For quite a number of years Paul kept several long-eared lanky deer hounds.

One summer, one of the hounds got into the habit of standing at the corner of the fence and howling. He didn't howl every night, but he needed no coaxing whenever the weather was just to his liking, and the moon shone clear and bright. Each howl was loud and long, and much shaded in tones, until it almost seemed as though the creature might be practicing grand opera.

Everyone seemed to be taking the dog's howling as a matter of course, except for the gentleman who occupied the second floor room in that corner of the hotel. This placed the nocturnal singer — or howler — almost beneath his windows. As he went to bed for the express purpose of sleeping, he wasn't at all in the mood to lie awake and listen to the howlings of an Adirondack hound. After being kept awake a few hours each of several nights the boarder, not knowing to whom the dog belonged, decided to complain to Mr. Smith.

In answer to his complaint, Paul said, "Why don't you shoot the dog if he bothers you so?"

The guest replied, "Why, I don't know! I don't think I'd like to do that."

Paul answered, "Well, I tell you now, I'd shoot him if he kept *me* awake."

That very night was bright and clear, with a full moon making it's slow way across the sky. The guest had just drifted off into his first deep sleep when the whole country-side began to echo with the dog's howling. The gentleman bounced out of his bed, and rushed to the open window. There just below him stood the dog on his two hind feet, with the front paws placed firmly on the top board of the fence, while he gazed and howled at the moon. With head up, and mouth open, the howls rolled from his throat in long drawn-out wails, while those that had gone out ahead still echoed and re-echoed from the surrounding hills.

The guest stood there watching and listening in helpless anger, with a feeling of great frustration upon him, for everything that he had tried on other nights to silence him had done no good. How he wished he knew *some* way to stop that racket! Then suddenly he remembered his morning's talk with Paul. He also remembred that he had a loaded gun in his room and it wasn't many minutes before he was aiming it, through the open window, at the dog. There was a flash and a report and, as the guest was a good marksman, and the distance short, the dog fell, to howl no more.

In the great silence that followed, the boarder became rather worried as to what the consequences might be in the morning when the owner found out his dog had been killed. But he needn't have worried. Although is was one of Paul's best dogs, and was valued at $50, Paul treated it as a joke, and he never let the guest know that the dog belonged to him.

Problems Too

Philemon King was one of the pioneer farmers in the town of Brighton. He was known everywhere as "Phil" and he and Paul Smith were neighbors and friends for many years.

Phil's family moved to the town of Brighton before he was twelve years old. In very early manhood he bought a small farm, and in 1857 he married Jane Quarters. Phil used to tell how he and his wife had, in their young days, worked at farming together bare-footed, to save wear and tear on shoes, which were expensive in those days.

Phil also said that he used to watch Paul Smith and, whenever he saw him go by with a new barrel of flour on his rig, he would hurry over and borrow a pailful of it.

In 1878 Phil bought a larger farm from Paul Smith, and agreed to pay $5,000 for it. Of course he didn't have the money, but Paul agreed to take his pay for the farm in milk, at five cents a quart. Phil was to have eight years to pay off the $5,000. However, Paul's establishment used so much milk that Phil had the farm paid for in five years.

In regard to the land-milk deal the story used to be told that there came a time when Paul accused Phil of adding water to the milk that he delivered to the hotel and refused to take any more milk from him. Phil declared the accusation to be false. When Paul would not back down and consent to take more milk, Phil sued him in an effort to make him live up to their agreement.

The case was to be tried in the Franklin County Court House at Malone. To support his claim Paul took with him four guides, who were near neighbors of both Phil and Paul, to serve as witnesses.

As the time for the trial drew near, and the people were taking their places in the court room, Phil went to Paul and asked, "Are those fellers over there your witnesses?"

"Yes," answered Paul, "they are."

"Then," said Phil, "I'll withdraw my suit, and I'll pay all the costs of the court, for I was planning to use them same witnesses myself."

They must have settled their case out of court and have made a new agreement, for as we have seen, Phil paid off the debt for the farm in record time.

No Hard Feelin's

One day in late summer Paul met Phil King and they stopped to visit a bit as was the custom in those days. (This idea of "stopping to visit" was not surprising, for all traveling was either done on foot, or with horses, or oxen as motive power.) Phil King was a farmer, and he and his wife each worked hard and long to "make ends meet."

When about ready to start on, Paul said, "Well, Phil, I suppose you and Jane are going to Malone to the fair. Ain't you?"

"No," replied Phil, "we've decided we can't go this year."

"You'd better go," said Paul. "If you don't go you'll miss a lot of fun. You and Jane have worked hard all summer, and *everybody* needs to have some pleasure. You'd better go along to the fair with me tomorrow."

Phil was deep in thought for a minute or so, and then said, "All right. We'll go."

When he reached home Phil said to his wife, "I met Paul, and he wants us to go to the fair with him tomorrow. He says we ought to go because we'll miss a lot of fun if we don't. So, by jinks, Jane, we'll go."

Neighborliness

Just because Paul Smith had bought 13,000 acres it did not stop him from buying more land when the opportunity came, if he considered it a bargain, and if it was in a desirable location. Therefore, through the years he bought several large areas containing hundreds of acres, much of it being forest land. But his ability to buy it and own it did not make Paul unneighborly.

Once when he had bought another large tract bordering the St. Regis Lakes, someone asked, "What are you planning to do with so much land, Paul? Are you going to have a preserve or make a private park?"

"Well," Paul answered, "I'm not going to build a fence around it, if that's what you mean. I don't fence my land, only just my garden, to keep the cows out. My land is free to everyone to travel around on as they please, to hunt on, or to fish on. All I ask is for them not to damage any timber, or start any fires."

You couldn't always tell what Paul was thinking, but he didn't appear to be in any great sympathy with one of his drivers, whom he found in the barn one day.

The driver, whom they all called "Uncle Dick" Noyes was reading a newspaper, and had just read aloud to the "gang" an advertisement announcing that Barnum's Circus would be in Malone the following week. Paul happened along just then, and with a wink at his companions, Dick turned to Paul and said, "I'd like to take a trip to Malone next week."

Paul had evidently heard, or read, about the circus, or he may have heard Dick reading the ad to the men. Anyhow, he proved his knowledge of the coming event when he answered, "Oh, yes! I know! You want to go to Malone so you can have a sick horse, and can stop over to see the circus, or a fair, or a horse race, or a camp-meeting, or a baby show, or anything else exciting that you want to see — it's always handy for you to have a sick horse." Paul turned to go back to the hotel, and left the gang laughing at the sheepish grin on Dick's face when he found he had been discovered at his own connivance.

It is quite likely, however, that "Uncle Dick" went to the circus. And that any others of the hotel staff that wanted to go and could be spared, were allowed time off to go to the circus, for P. T. Barnum, owner of the circus, and Paul Smith were good friends for many years.

CHAPTER X

Workin' Side By Side

It was about 1878 that Paul was having a large addition built on his hotel. He was walking around one day as he usually did, to see how the work was progressing, and he found they were just about ready to raise a heavy post, or beam, to fit into the frame. There were several workmen standing close by and Paul asked the "boss mechanic" why he had so many men around just to raise one post.

The boss's reply was, "Because I need 'em."

Paul looked at the post, and at the place in the frame into which the post was to be set. Then he looked at the boss, and said, "I'll bet you I can take *one* man and we'll raise that beam and put it into its place." The boss was real quick to take Paul up on his bet.

There was quite a group of men standing around watching the work and as Paul looked out at them he saw his brother-in-law, Charles Martin, among them. Paul waved his arm, and called for him to come and help him. And those two men, Paul and Charles, did indeed raise the post and put it into place in the frame.

The Smith family had been enlarging, and modernizing, their hotel plan, both inside and out, for several years. As part of those plans they had decided the barns and stables must be moved a considerable distance farther away from the hotel.

As soon as the hotel had closed its summer season in 1885 a crew of men, who were supposed to be skilled in the moving of buildings, arrived from Keeseville, more than 45 miles away.

It was to be quite a job for the times, as the buildings had to be separated, moved and put together again in the new location, on new foundations.

Weather or Not

Wherever, and whenever, one builds in the Adirondacks the weather is quite apt to be a hindrance, and so it was that fall. The season was getting late for building, for snow could be expected soon. It was already October, and they were trying to lay a new foundation. In those days cement blocks were not available, at least in the north country. Therefore, native stones had to be picked from the fields, and forest lands for such use. With such stones, all shapes and sizes, care had to be taken to fit each stone to those about it, so that a level solid wall would arise; the stones must be so chosen and laid that the wall had at least one even face. Cement or mortar was not often used in the making of barn foundations; and even the foundations of many houses were laid without mortar to a depth of three or four feet below the surface of the ground. Above such a depth it was expected that the ground would freeze during the winter months, and so cause the freezing of potatoes, vegetables and apples that were stored in the cellar. Therefore, from there on up a solid, air-tight, wall was built by using plenty of mortar to fill all the spaces and crevices between the stones.

There had been a cold dreary rain for several days, which delayed the work greatly. On one of those mornings Paul looked around at the cloudy skies, the pouring rain, the muddy ground, and the wet and gloomy men. Then he turned to them and said, "Well, there's no two ways about it. We must be a long ways from purgatory, if what they say about that place is true. They say it never rains anywhere near there. But it rains all the time here."

Day after day, whenever the weather allowed, the work went on, until finally all but the last building, which was the largest and heaviest of them all, had been successfully moved, and reset on their new foundations.

It was then that real trouble started. The equipment wasn't heavy enough for the job, and it kept breaking down. The weather grew colder, and snow showers began to come. The men became discouraged and wanted to quit. The foreman went to Paul and told him he thought they had better leave the remainder of the job until spring. That idea didn't fit in with Paul's plans at all and it gave him the blues just to think of it. He called the group of men together, and said, "If you fellows will stick to it, and finish this job, when it's done I'll give you a gallon of good whiskey, besides your pay, to celebrate. The men were delighted with that offer, and went back to their work with renewed zeal.

One morning they found they had more work to do than they had expected, for they discovered that part of a large bank of dirt had to be dug away and moved, to make room for that last foundation, in order to set the building just where Paul wanted it. It looked like all that extra work couldn't be done in the time left to them, for winter was so close that every hour counted. Paul, as usual, was out early to see how things were going. When the new problem was presented to him, he went and hunted up a shovel, stepped in with the other men and went to work. All day he shoveled dirt onto the wagons, and it seemed that his presence and example inspired all the men to work with new vim and vigor. By nightfall *that* job was done and there wasn't a man among them who had shoveled more dirt than Paul.

The weather also cooperated by warming up and melting the snow. And just at dusk, a few nights later, the building was safely located on its new foundation.

Paul was on hand to see the job finished, and he straightened up and shouted, "Hooray, boys! Hooray! You did it! Hooray!" Then he hurried to the house to tell Mrs. Smith and their sons.

It was a happy, noisy gang of men that sat about the fire that evening. Many were the jokes that were told, and the stories that were swapped during those hours. Paul was so pleased that he wanted to add to the men's pleasure by bringing the promised whiskey out right then. But the foreman had had experience with those men, and he knew pretty well what whiskey was likely to do to them, so he advised Paul to wait until morning; "For," he said, "some of 'em might forget to wind their watches tonight, and so might not be up, and able to start home on time in the morning."

The men, of course, didn't know of the conversation between Paul and the foreman. They had hoped he would bring on the whiskey during the evening. But when bed time came and nothing had been said about it, they went to bed feeling rather glum. That feeling was still with them in the morning, and they were a sober-looking crowd as they washed, before eating what would be their last meal on that job.

Just as the wash-up job was completed Paul came in with several bottles which had "Old Crow" labels on them. There went up a cheer from the dry throats and the men were eager to sample the "Old Crow" before breakfast. When the sample drinks were finally passed around they all expressed great satisfaction, for the whiskey was a better quality than most of the men were used to. By the time they had their equipment loaded and the two wagons were ready to leave, they were all in the mood to drink to the health of Mr. Smith, all his family and all the available hired help.

The bottles must have been freely passed around during the

nine-mile trip to Bloomingdale, for it proved to be a lively trip. However, they did manage to reach that village without a mishap.

At Bloomingdale, the foreman looked his crew over, and saw that he must either leave several of the men there or would have to tie them to the wagons if he didn't want them falling out on the way home. As soon as the wagons were stopped the men climbed, or tumbled, out and made themselves "comfortable" on the sidewalk, or the nearest doorstep. They were all pretty well under the influence of "Old Crow," every drop of which had disappeared down some thirsty throat.

The foreman, who wasn't a drinking man, decided it would be easier, and cheaper, to leave some of the men in Bloomingdale, than to buy the rope that would be needed to tie them safely into the wagons. He asked for the help of some of the men who had gathered 'round, and they dragged, or carried, the men one by one into the stables of the old St. Armand House, whose proprietor at the time was Captain James Pierce. The drunken men, most of whom were sleeping noisily, were deposited on the hay which had been spread out on the barn floor. With a blanket or two to cover them they were left to sleep the rest of the day and through the night.

The foreman made arrangements for one of the teams and wagons to be cared for at the stables, to provide transportation when the men were fit to travel. Then he went on his way with his equipment and a few of the men who were still able to travel.

No doubt the foreman and his gang always remembered that fall job at Paul Smith's and its grand finale.

Settlin' Trouble

Paul Smith had ways all his own of settling disputes among his help and sometimes he would try a little "bluff game" on them which quite often worked.

One evening he had started to walk to the stables, as he often did, and he happened to meet "Uncle" Dick Noyes who was on his way up to the house. As soon as he reached Paul, Dick started to complain, and said that Jake Johnson, who was the stable foreman, had taken some article of Dick's out of Dick's box-stall and had used it. (In those early days there was an unwritten law that this should not be done. Each teamster on a job had his own tools for cleaning and caring for the horses which he drove. No one else was supposed to meddle with them ever.) "And," Dick continued, "if that's the way Jake Johnson is going to run things around here I'd better pack up right *now*, and *go*."

"Well," Paul said, "don't fret about it. I'll go right along down there, and I'll give him hell;" and he stepped along toward the stables.

When Paul reached the horse barn he hunted up Jake and stood and talked with him about several different matters. But he didn't mention Dick's name, nor anything that Dick had said.

As Paul was on his way back to the house he could see Noyes just starting on his return trip to the barn, and Paul hurried on so he would be far enough from the stables to be out of Johnson's hearing when he and Noyes met. When the two men had come close together they each stopped, and Paul said, "Well, I gave him a d____ good blowing up. Everything should be all right now."

Dick looked real pleased, and as he entered the stables he gave Jake a defiant look which seemed to say, "Now! Will you do that again?"

Braggin' on the Boss

Paul Smith's help held him in high regard, each in his own way, and they were most generally ready to "brag on their boss" a little. George Meserve, one of Paul's teamsters, made a good showing along that line one day.

George had been to a station on the Chateaugay Railroad (supposedly to Loon Lake), and was on his way back to Paul Smith's with a coach load of several young men as passengers. It was their first visit to the mountains, and they were full of fun, vigor and questions.

The "boys" took their seats in the coach, some on the inside and some on the outside. Their exuberance would not allow them to be quiet anywhere for long. They did not want to wait until they got to Paul Smith's before the began to get acquainted so they soon demanded that Meserve should tell them "all about Paul Smith."

"Well," began George, "he keeps things to sell. Lots of things. You can get most any kind of thing you want, from a one-cent postage stamp up to one hundred cords of stove wood. Or you could get a thousand feet of lumber, providin' you've got the necessary amount of good clean money to pay for it. Paul don't take dirty money for anything he sells you. But he'll give you plenty of fresh air and pure water. He throws them in for good measure."

One of the young men asked, "What kind of looking man is this Paul Smith? I can only stay up here one night, but I've heard so much about him that I've just got to meet the man and talk with him."

Meserve gave him a good description of Paul and then added, "As for talkin' with him, if *he* ever gets talkin' with *you* you'll never forget it. Talk is very cheap with him."

"I think," said one of the fellows, "if talk is cheap, it is about the only thing around his place that is cheap. Isn't it?"

"Well," George replied, "I can tell you you won't stay with him long unless you're pretty well heeled. He isn't in there just for his health." And then he added, "Why, he owns all this land, as far as you can see, on both sides of the road." The truth was that Paul didn't own any of the land that they could see, but as they had no way of knowing it they believed all Meserve told them.

Another one of the passengers spoke up, and said, "Anyhow, I noticed that Paul Smith isn't getting *all* the money that's floating around up here. Ferd Chase, at the Loon Lake House must be getting some of it for I noticed they left fifteen trunks at the Loon Lake station marked for Chase's Hotel."

"Oh! That's nothing," bragged Meserve. "If we don't handle twice that many, each trip, every day, we think we ain't doing much business at Paul's."

Landlord, How Much?

It is quite likely that every hotel keeper receives amusing letters. Paul Smith was no exception and he kept one on file for many years. An exact copy of it follows:

Westfield, N.J.

_____1888

"Dear Sir,

My wife and her mother, my three little girls, aged ten, eight and six, and the baby, aged one year, and myself will go to the Adirondacks. What would be your terms for one week and how much for three to six weeks? Can we hire a horse by the week at reasonable terms, or by the day or half day? And how much is washing? We would like to know your principles on canned vegetables. We like fish and eggs or lamb and milk, and suppose your ordinary bill of fare is abundantly good enough for us. How high is your house and

what do you see from it? How could we arrange about going
in from railroad and at what expense, if you please? Is your
house old or new? At our last place they charged us $30 for
the same crowd, except that we had another woman instead
of my wife's mother. I write two or three other places by
this mail.

Yours truly,

_____

One wonders what Paul's reply may have been. It should have
been interesting.

CHAPTER XI

To and From the Hotel

As the number of guests increased and the hotel was enlarged, Paul continued to add to the number of horses and rigs until he had a great many, among them a stage coach for a six-horse-hitch. And, as has often been told, for a time he had six black horses which he used for the daytime trips, and six pure whites for the night time driving. He also finally acquired, and sometimes used, an 8 horse stage coach or "tally-ho."

In 1868, the Whitehall and Plattsburgh Railroad finished a 20 mile stretch of railway line, that ran in a south-westerly direction from Plattsburgh to Point of Rocks or Ausable River Station. This line was extended some miles up-river to a point near the outlet for the Roger's iron mines that were in that area. It was natural that the railroad began to be used more and more as a passenger route. The name given to the station was "Rogers," and no community was ever built up around it. Since it stood by itself, and since many of the people for miles around had to go through Ausable Forks Village in order to reach the station, practically everyone spoke of going to the train at Ausable Forks. It was at that station that Paul Smith picked up and delivered a great many of his guests in those early days. And they always spoke of it as going to Ausable Forks, as we shall.

The station was just about 42 miles from Paul Smith's. The roads were dirt roads — narrow, crooked, hilly, stretches of corduroy, muddy or dusty according to the weather. There were about three miles of plank road which the Western Plank Road Co. had built in 1850 which extended from Franklin Falls to the line dividing the towns of Franklin and Black Brook, in which the town Ausable Forks is located.

Usually a stop for meals, and sometimes an exchange of horses, was made at Franklin Falls, which was about half way between Paul's and the railroad station. Franklin Falls in those days was a

117

thriving community, with a large modern hotel. The hotel catered mainly to transient trade, as it was located on the Port Kent-Hopkinton Turnpike. Undoubtedly the passenger passing through today would say, "I don't believe it." In 1871 one traveler took time after dinner to count the names on the hotel register, and found there were already 1500 names for that season which was then only half gone.

In 1874, the railroad line from Plattsburgh to Rogers was again extended several miles to Ausable Forks, bringing the station that much closer to Paul's.

In 1887, the Chateaugay Railroad between Plattsburgh and Saranac Lake was finally completed and the first train was run from Plattsburgh to Saranac Lake on December 5th that year. This line was later sold to the Delaware and Hudson Company.

Dr. W. Seward Webb of New York, who was a son-in-law of Wm. H. Vanderbilt of that city, had become impressed by what he felt was a great need for a railroad running from Malone on the North, through the Adirondacks to Herkimer on the South. He not only saw the need for it, but to him it seemed quite possible to accomplish. As such a road would open a new route of travel between New York and Montreal he took his plan to the New York Central Railroad officials but he couldn't get them interested in the idea. However, he still thought the area needed such a road and he applied to the state for a grant for the land for the right-of-way. But he was again refused. Dr. Webb seems to have been a man who didn't discourage easily, and he decided that he, himself, would build the railroad, and he immediately started buying the land that would be needed for the right-of-way.

The work on the roadbed was begun in 1890. On July 1st, 1893, the first train traveled from Malone to Lake Clear and on over the spur to Saranac Lake. The road from Lake Clear to Herkimer was finished soon after that. Some people called this railroad a "rich man's foolishness," and dubbed it "Webb's Golden Chariot Route." However, Webb had the last laugh, for the New York Central people soon saw its value, and they made arrangements with Webb to use the line, and still later on they bought it outright.

Driver, How Fast?

With guests coming and going in several directions, it was sometimes necessary to make trips to all three stations, Ausable Forks, Malone and Plattsburgh, on the same day. Therefore, Paul needed more and more horses and, if more horses, then more barns were needed, of course. Eventually he had barns for 50 to 60 horses, and drivers sufficient to care for them. Each driver had his own team, or teams, for which he was responsible. He was supposed to keep the horses fed, watered and groomed, their stables clean and harnesses and rigs clean and in good condition. In that way Paul knew whom to praise, or blame, for the condition of either the horses or rigs.

Through the years Paul had some horses that became famous for their speed. His neighbors, far and near, gave up all hope of having any horses that would pass Paul's. Some of them were spoken of familiarly as the "Robin horse," the "chestnut trotters," the "Dart mare," the "little black ponies," and then there were "Ralph and Harry." It was said of them, "No better, kinder, or prettier horses ever traveled the roads." Paul loved his horses, and fairly often would made a station trip himself, just for the sake of driving or riding behind some of them.

Paul expected his drivers to use discretion in the matter of speed, and he, too, was generally pretty careful along that line. There was nothing he liked better than the feel of a pair of reins in his hands, as he guided a pair of fast trotters along the highway. The highways were dirt roads, with now and then a strip of corduroy, or at the best a few miles of plank road. Paul was never satisfied until he passed every rig which he overtook.

For a few years Paul had a pair of black horses of which he was especially fond. They were quite speedy and were capable of great endurance. Paul often wondered how much they could do, and one day he decided to find out.

He had been to the Point of the Rocks railroad station, near Ausable Forks, with the "Blacks" on a light rig. He had a friend with him who was also one of his hotel guests. The weather, the day, the company, perhaps just life in general, all seemed to combine to put Paul in the right mood for daring. Anyhow, he suddenly decided to put his team to the test.

As they started out the horses seemed to share Paul's mood, for they needed no urging. To travel from Ausable Forks to Paul Smith's one is climbing into the mountains. Since there is a rise in altitude of nearly 1100 feet between the two places, it is no surprise to find a few long and fairly steep hills. Part of the distance between "the Forks" and Franklin Falls was of the then-modern "plank road" variety, the rest was dirt, except for occasional short stretches that were of corduroy, as otherwise the road in those spots would be very muddy in wet weather.

The "Blacks" were eager to go, and Paul let them have their way pretty much, and seeing horses and driver were all of the same mind they went speedily forward.

The hills must have had to be taken at a walk, even for that team, but when they struck the miles of plank road it is very possible that they exceeded the speed that used to be spoken of as "going two-forty of the plank road." So they traveled from the Forks, up to Black Brook, past the Coal Kilns Settlements, onward to Franklin Falls, along the river to Bloomingdale, and beyond, and finally stopped before Paul's hotel.

The time in which the trip was made has long since been forgotten, but Paul was triumphant, for he had broken all past records, and had made a new one which he thought would never be equalled in all time to come. And it never was. The Blacks "were pretty well warmed up," but suffered no ill effects.

Paul was overjoyed. But the peak was taken off his joy a.little while later when Mrs. Smith heard about it and told him plainly what she thought about it. Perhaps Paul stopped then to realize what he would have said if one of his drivers had ever tried such a stunt.

Stage Coaches and Trains

Absolutely no mention is made as to how those men who first came to hunt and fish while they stopped at Paul Smith's Hunter's Home, got from wherever they called home to the Adirondacks.

At the time when Paul Smith set up his boarding establishment there were stagecoach lines between some principal points to aid those who must travel. Railroads and trains had been invented just a few years before, and the Northern Railroad from Ogdensburg to Malone was built shortly after 1845. This did not do too much for Paul Smith's area, though, for most of his guests at that time seemed to come from the east and the south. From those directions no railroad had yet come nearer to the Adirondacks than Whitehall, close to the southern tip cf Lake Champlain. Boats were used wherever available and, having arrived at Whitehall, one could transfer to a boat and travel northward on Lake Champlain to Plattsburgh, using the greater part of the day for the trip to Port Kent, or some other nearby docking point. From there, there was still the trip to be made "inland" to whatever point one's desires were taking him.

Since the middle or late 1820s, there had been a stagecoach line between Port Kent and Hopkinton. This route passed through Black Brook, Franklin Falls, Merrillsville, Loon Lake and on northwestward to Hopkinton. The Lovering Place which Paul rented for his first few years as a hotel keeper was already a well-established stagecoach inn on that route. And the Hunter's Home that he later built on the nearby property that he bought was also located on that same "turnpike." Therefore, the matter of transportation for his guests at Hunter's Home was as well taken care of as could be expected for the times.

You See the Strangest Sights

In the days when the Paul Smith guests had to be transported 40 miles or more to and from the railroad station, Paul was riding up with a stage-load of new guests.

To make the trip pleasanter the men were talking and joking. Paul, as usual, had been doing quite a lot of good-natured bragging about the pure air and water, and the healthy climate of the Adirondacks. That particular time he ended his remarks by saying, "Why, it is so healthy up here that nobody ever dies."

That sounded good, and Paul seemed to have stated an indisputable fact, so the talk took a new direction. But it was not long until they came to a cemetery. As they were passing it one of the men who had been taking a prominent part in the conversation was quick to notice it, and he promptly said, "Mr. Smith, look there!" and he winked at the other passengers. "If no one ever dies around here how do you account for this cemetery?" The men all laughed at that, for they were sure they had the best of Paul.

But Paul answered without any hesitancy, and as though they all ought to have known it before, "Why!" he said, "All those bodies buried out there were sent up here from New York City. We sent down there for them so we could have a cemetery, for everyone seemed to think we should have one. We may *live* in the backwoods up here, but we believe in being in style if we can."

Short Cuts Can Be Long

Many men who work themselves "up from the sticks" get proud and arrogant — much set up with their own importance — to speak it plainly, they become just plain snobs. They are never content unless they think everyone else has "set them on a pedestal" where they may be properly admired. We have all met some of those people, but there was never anything like that about Paul Smith.

Though he had come up from "rags to riches," and, though he counted some of the nation's richest and most noted as his friends, Paul Smith never pushed himself forward as if to say, "I'm here! Don't forget me! Just see who I am! See what I have done!" Many a time it seemed as though he wanted to hide his identity, not because of shame, but for pure modesty's sake. He *had* to know that he had become a famous man and that his name was known far and wide. He appeared to feel that if he admitted to being "Paul Smith" he would be bragging.

It so happened that late one afternoon, when the old Northern Adirondack Railroad was being built from Santa Clara to the first "Paul Smith's Station" near Buck Mountain, Paul stopped at a lumber camp some distance above Spring Cove.

Paul had been driving home from St. Regis Falls and, thinking to shorten the distance, had followed an old lumber road which he felt sure would bring him out near his own place. But, as there were several lumbering roads in the area he managed to get onto a wrong one, and he followed it so far that when he found out his mistake it was too late for him to reach home that night. Therefore, when he came to a large lumber camp he stopped to ask for food and lodging.

It was Saturday and during the afternoon all the men had gone out to the "Settlement" except the man who was the camp cook. He seemed real glad to see Paul and to have company and, with true backwoods hospitality, made Paul welcome, though he had no idea who his caller might be. It is quite likely that Paul supposed the cook knew who he was, and, therefore, did not identify himself. And so the evening began.

As he told about the event afterward the cook said, "I got supper and he seemed to enjoy it, and complimented me on my cookin'. After we finished eatin' we just sat and talked, and I tell you I didn't get lonesome that night. He told me a lot of funny stories, and he told about things that happened when he was workin' on a farm, and other stories about choppin' in the woods."

"I never had a better visit with anyone than I had with him that night. He had a good supply of first class cigars, and he wasn't a bit slow about passin' 'em over to me. Man! But they was good smokin'!"

"I wondered some who he was, but I hated to ask him. I decided it didn't matter much about his name for he was sure one grand feller. I thought he was prob'ly a jobber, and asked him if he had a lumber job. He said, "'No! But I lumber some every winter.' When I asked him what he did in the summer, he just said, 'I keep boarders.'"

"In the mornin', when we was havin' breakfast, he said, 'If you're in these parts again next summer why don't you come up to my place on Sunday, or any time you have a day off? Bring another one of the boys with you and have dinner with me.'"

"Then he went on, 'I'll show you my garden and I'll have my boatman let you take a boat, and you can row up through the lakes, and see a lot of nice camps that wealthy people spend their summers in. I'll introduce you to some of my girls. Maybe you might catch onto one of them, for I have more than 80 girls workin' for me every summer.'"

"Then," the cook continued, "I said, who be you anyway? And he said, in a sort of off-handed way, 'Paul Smith.'"

"Talk about surprised! Man! Since I've been around these parts I've heard a lot about Paul Smith, but I never had any idea he was the kind of a feller that would set and talk to a common feller like a camp cook, in such a friendly way, just as though he was a workin' man himself."

"When he was ready to leave he shook hands with me, and wanted to pay for the food and lodging for himself and horses. But I wouldn't let him. But I did take a big handful of those cigars that he handed out to me."

Some Drivers Stay a Long Time

The character of a man who employs help can be fairly well determined by the length of time any one man, or woman, works for him. Using that as a rule one has the right to believe that Paul Smith was not a disagreeable man to have as an employer.

Among those who worked for Paul long periods of time were:

Mary Ryan, who put in 23 years of work for Paul, sometimes as waitress, at other times as chambermaid, cook, or general supervisor of the house.

Henry Ryan had charge of the General Store for at least 17 years.

Charles Cutler was assistant clerk in the store for more than 12 years.

John Corbett, from Fort Edward, had charge of the bar for 11 years.

George Meserve was considered one of the leading stage, or coach drivers in the United States. He drove for Paul at least 12 years, part of that time driving a six-horse team on a coach to and from the hotel and road stations, and on pleasure outings with the guests.

Henry Prentice worked for Paul for more than 12 years. He was head machinist in the mills, electric plants and water works.

Presumably there were other long term workers whose names were not kept on record.

To offset the satisfactory long-term help there were always some who were unsatisfactory. Paul had his own way of dealing with them. He always hated to "call them down," and some might say he had queer ways of doing so. But those ways usually seemed to be effective, even though there might not be many words used. His help generally accepted his word as law with no back talk, or argument. If it became necessary to fire a person, he would often say, "I've got to give you your nine cents." And he would pay him off and let him go.

Some a Short Time

One summer Paul had a man driving one of his best outfits, which consisted of a pair of sleek, fat horses, shiny harnesses, and a new-style Glens Falls covered buckboard on springs.

It didn't take that driver long to discover that the team of horses could travel, and from the day of that discovery he seemed to fear that "grass would grow under the horses' feet" if they didn't hasten on.

That driver also had too much of a liking for the "spirits" that are supposed to cheer and, whenever he was sent out, he always managed to fortify himself with enough of those "spirits" to keep him from getting lonesome between stops.

One morning in late August, Paul was taking his morning walk about the grounds. It was a crisp, frosty morning and he was feeling a bit low as he realized that the summer season was drawing near its close. Those busy, companionable, enjoyable summers! How he hated to have each one end!

As he went up the slope from the boathouse Paul noticed a team, carriage and driver waiting near the front door of the hotel, to take a party out. He couldn't fail to see that the horses were thin, and poorly groomed, the harnesses were dirty and needed oiling, the metal portions were showing rust and the carriage was marred, scratched and needed washing. Paul went nearer and, beginning at the hind wheels, examined the whole outfit thoroughly, ending his inspection at the horses' heads. Then he stepped back to the driver, and with the piercing look which was peculiar to him when in such a mood, he sternly informed the driver that the whole outift, horses, carriage and harnesses, under his management were "going to hell just as fast as they could go."

"Well," the driver said, in an argumentative tone, "I can't help it! I ain't to blame!"

"Oh, hell, no! *You* ain't to blame for *anything*!" said Paul. And he turned and walked off.

The driver knew that, though Paul had gone, he would not forget. And that it was more than likely that he would be around before the day was done to give him "his nine cents."

Another Nine Cents

Just about every summer Paul had to take on one or more new teamsters to replace some who failed to return.

One year, on a rainy day, one of those new drivers failed to return from some trip as quickly as Paul thought he should have.

When he remarked to the other men, "I wonder what's keeping that fellow," one of the men replied, "Probably he's laying over for the rain."

Paul said, "Huh! I'd like to have him lay over for the rain and know about it. He'd get his nine cents darn quick."

Bottled Goods Can Be Dangerous

One day one of the drivers, who was called Chet, was sent to take a party of people to the Ausable Forks railroad station, 42 miles away.

Before he started back next day he managed to get a supply of bottled goods that would keep him from getting too dry on the way home.

Just at dusk that evening one of the stable men saw Chet drive into the carriage house, and when he looked out a few minutes later he was driving in again. He couldn't think what could be the trouble, and he called to some of the other men who were near by. They watched as Chet drove the team across the carriage-house floor, out through the open back doorway, around the stable to the front of the building, then in at the open front door again, making a complete circuit. The "boys" thought that was quite a joke, and they kept watch while he made a half-dozen, or so, of such trips. For the sake of the horses they stopped him on his next round, and asked him what kind of a performance he was trying to put on.

Chet was quite out of patience, and disgusted, and in a thick voice answered, "I'm trying to get away from that devilish covered bridge. I don't know what's the matter with it. It's after me! I drive through it all right and go a little ways, and then the dumb thing is right there in front of me again. It must be haunted or something." In the state of mind to which his bottled goods had gotten him, he thought he was driving through the covered bridge over the Ausable River many miles away.

The men thought it such a joke that it was told around the grounds, until some time late in the evening Paul heard the story.

Next morning after Chet's mind and his vision had both cleared Paul hunted him up, and said, "You drive through too many covered bridges to handle my teams." Then as he gave Chet "his nine cents" he added, "I don't want any more covered bridge drivers around here."

Personal Transportation

After Paul built his new hotel on St. Regis Lake he began to acquire horses, and the number increased as his needs grew. Saddle horses, for his own need and pleasure, as well as for his guests, were also among his purchases, and he was soon spending many hours a week riding around the countryside. He rode so easily he almost seemed to be a part of the horse and it may be that he had done a great deal of riding as a youngster in Vermont. As he rode, Paul always had a greeting for everyone whom he met or passed, and a special wave and greeting for the children at play as he passed their homes.

Using horses as he traveled from place to place, must have been so much easier and swifter than formerly, that Paul undoubtedly thought that he was making as much speed as he would ever attain on these country roads. He probably never imagined that there would some day be something more speedy to use, and that he, Paul Smith, would be the first one in his own area to own such a vehicle. But that time came and his flaming red automobile was the first car that many of the inhabitants of this area ever saw.

As he traveled at the excessive speeds of 15 or 20 miles an hour in those first cars, he still greeted men, women and children as he had always done. Every one in the family lined up at windows, doors, or outside, to see and to wave as he went speeding by.

CHAPTER XII

Stories: Long and Short

How Many Otises?

Edward Derby, one of Paul Smith's early friends, conducted a grocery store in Bloomingdale. One day Paul and Henry Otis, who was a neighbor of very small stature, went to Bloomingdale and stopped at Derby's store. They found several men sitting around inside; among them was Jim Cross, who was six feet and four inches tall, and accordingly large.

Derby picked up a pencil and started busily figuring. He found himself too busy to wait on any new customers, so the men stood and watched as he figured and crossed out, and then started over again. This he did several times and apparently could get no satisfactory answer to whatever his problem was.

After a while Paul said, "What you figuring, Ed?"

Derby replied, "I'm figuring to see if I cut up Jim Cross how many Otises I could make out of him."

Pay Up

Edward Derby later went into the hotel business and ran the Saranac Inn for some years. Paul Smith used to enjoy telling the following story concerning those days.

A couple of men came to the Inn to stay overnight. The next morning, after paying their bills, they got into a boat to go on farther down the lake. In discussing their stay at the Inn one of the men said, "My bill for the night was $12.00."

The other man said, "Is that so? My bill was $20.00 They made a mistake! They charged me too much."

The men, though traveling separately, had arrived at the hotel, and had left it, at the same time. So they took out their two bills and in comparing them found they had had the same privileges. Realizing a mistake had been made they turned their boat around and hurried back to the Inn.

They found Derby in the office, and the first man said, "How is this, sir? You have charged my friend $20.00 for the same services for which you charged me $12.00."

Derby said, "Let me see your bill."

The man handed him the bill, and, after studying it for a minute Derby said, "Why, yes! I see where the trouble is. You are right. This *is* a mistake. *Your* bill should have been $20.00 too, instead of $12.00. Just give me $8.00 more and everything will be straightened out."

In seeing the way Derby figured it the man was too amazed to say a word, but hunted through his pockets until he found the extra $8.00 which he paid and again they started on their journey.

Don't Make Me Laugh

Henry Otis seems not to have been the only man (nor the only Otis) of small stature in the area, for Paul used to tell about big Jim Cross and Joshua Otis. Joshua was only five feet tall, while Jim was 6 feet 4 inches.

Paul would say, "One evening Cross and Josh Otis and a few guides were telling stories and Cross and Otis each did a lot of bragging about his own ability as a great hunter.

"Josh finally got provoked, and he said, '*You! You!* You think you're a big hunter just because you're a big man. Why, Jim, I've a good notion to put you in my pocket.'"

"That created a good laugh I tell you; when you looked at the difference in the size of the two men."

"But Big Jim wasn't to be beat even on blarney, and he said, 'Well, Josh, if you do you'll have more brains in your pocket than you've got in your head.'"

"That ended the bragging for that night."

Expensive Advice

"Andy McTavish used to work here," said Paul, "and he had a spell when he was 'no feelin' just weel' as he said, and so he went to see the doctor. After he'd stated his troubles the doctor said, 'What do you drink?'"

"'Whuskey,' Andy replied."

"The doctor said, 'How much?'"

"'Oh, mayhap a bottle a day,' was Andy's reply."

"Then the doc said, 'Do you smoke?'"

"'Yis,' says Andy."

"The doc asked, 'How much?' "

" 'About two ounces a day,' says Andy again."

" 'Well,' the doctor said, 'You give up drinking whiskey, and using tobacco and I think you will soon be all right.' "

"Andy picked up his cap and made for the door, reaching it in just three long strides. As he opened it the doctor called out, "Andy, I know I didn't give you any medicine, but I did give you some advice, and you haven't paid for it.' "

"Andy was stopped on the threshold, and looking back at the doctor he said, 'Full weel I know that, but Ah'm no takin' the advice.' And he turned to the door and slamming it shut behind him went down the steps and set off toward home."

If You Can't Eat 'Em, Mount 'Em

As has been said, Paul Smith got his stories wherever he could find them. And one of the choice ones that he delighted to tell was about an unfortunate mistake that Phil King made one summer's day.

As Paul told it, the story went like this, "There was my old friend, Phil King. He was a good man and a good farmer. Like most of us men he left all the house work as well as all the cooking up to Jane, his good wife. She was a number one cook, and most any meal she got up was fit for a prince."

"One day, a few years back, Doug Martin stopped at Phil's place and gave him a number of nice trout he had just caught."

"Phil was real pleased with 'em and thanked Doug a-plenty, for Jane as well as for himself. Phil loved trout and he started into the house thinking what a real good dinner Jane would make with those beauties. Phil had forgotten for the minute that Jane had gone off that morning and wouldn't be back in time to fuss much for supper. But she had partly got supper ready so it wouldn't take long to finish it when she got home."

"Phil looked around at what Jane had started and decided the fish would make a good addition to the meal. And he made up his mind he would cook 'em himself and surpirse Jane. He had done some cooking the winter before while he was in a logging camp for awhile, and he had felt sort of proud of his success. So he rolled up his sleeves, washed his hands and went to work."

"It took Phil a while to hunt up a piece of pork for fat. And then he had to hunt some more to find the flour to roll the trout in. In due time he had a platter of as nice looking, well-browned, trout as you ever see."

"It was just about time for Jane to come home, so Phil went outside and waited for her. He was so excited about cooking the fish, and they looked and smelled so good, that he was like a little boy. And he told Jane all about them before they really got into the house. Jane recognized the boyishness and told him, even before she saw the fish, that he had done fine. And when she did see 'em they looked so beautiful that she praised him some more. She fussed around a little and pretty soon everything was ready and they set down to eat."

"Phil looked at the platter of fish almost lovingly. And he was so tickled to have his wife, who was one of the best cooks in the Adirondacks, praise his cooking that he hardly knew what to do. So he just sat for a minute and gazed first at Jane and then at the fish. Then real quick he said, 'Say, Jane, I thought we had a plenty of flour. I had an *awful* time to find any.'"

"Jane was real surprised, and she said, 'Why, we have got a plenty of flour. We got a new barrel of flour just yesterday.'"

"Phil said, 'That's what I thought, but I looked all over the pantry and couldn't find it. But I finally found a little in a small sack.'"

"'In a sack?' Jane says. And she got up and hurried into the pantry. Phil followed her and she showed him the new barrel of flour setting there in the corner of the closet, and there was a small tin can setting on top of it. The barrel hadn't been opened but Jane told Phil that what flour was left from the old barrel was in the tin can."

"Phil looked around bewildered like, and then he picked up a small dark brown paper sack, and he said, 'Here's the flour I used.'"

"Jane took one look and then set down quick in the kitchen chair, all done in with laughing.'"

"Phil watched her for a minute, and then said, 'Well, what *is* the stuff?'"

"'Oh, Phil!' she gasped. 'That's plaster of Paris. Surely you didn't . . .'"

"'Surely I did!' said Phil. 'That's just what I used. I rolled those trout in *that*.'"

"Course Phil was disappointed, and I guess Jane was too, not to eat those fish for they both liked 'em. But Jane went to work, and pretty soon she had something else ready for supper in place of the fish."

No Dogs Here

Back in the days of the latter half of the 19th century just about every family in Paul Smith's town kept from one to a half dozen dogs, most of them being hounds and Paul usually had more than anyone else.

As supervisor of his town of Brighton, Paul was attending a meeting of the Board of Supervisors in Malone, the county seat. Someone brought up the matter of the advisability of assessing a tax on dogs, and they asked Paul what he would think about it for his town.

"Why," he said, "I don't know as we *need* it. There ain't any dogs in my town."

The men all laughed derisively, and one said, "What do you mean, no dogs in your town, Mr. Smith?"

"No!" declared Paul "I mean it. There ain't a dog in the whole town of Brighton."

That settled the dog-tax question for that session, and nothing more was said about it — then. But, after the meeting was adjourned, first one and then another of the men joked to Paul about there being no dogs in his town.

Then one man said to another, "I'm thinking Paul Smith put it pretty strong when he said there are no dogs in his town."

"Yes! I know he did," said the second man. "I traveled all over the country last summer, and I saw more dogs in the town of Brighton than I did anywhere else."

Of course, the conversation was being held in Paul's hearing and for his benefit, so he interrupted and said, "Those dogs you saw last summer didn't *live* in Brighton. They were just there on a visit from other towns. The people up in the North Woods are neighborly and so are their dogs."

Only One Holiday

One day a certain young man went to Paul Smith's hotel to apply for a job. When he gave his name Paul recognized him as a young man who had the reputation of being rather careless about appearing for work, but he would take a day, or a part of a day, off any time the idea happened to appeal to him.

Paul looked at the young man steadily for a minute or two, then he said, "Young feller, if you want to work for me I can give you a job. *But* I'll expect you to work steady, every day all summer. It's got to be understood that you can't go off fishin', or to the circus, or to celebrate some holiday every time the fit happens to take you. You'd better know now that the only holiday we celebrate around here," and he winked at one of the men standing near, "is election day. Yes sir! Election Day in the afternoon."

Women and the Weather

One Sunday afternoon Paul was out for a walk with a couple of male guests who had arrived the day before. This was their first visit to the mountains. It was a beautiful sunny day, and it was a joy to stroll along the shaded path that branched off from the road, and led through the garden to the further side of a small nearby pond.

When they reached the garden they found the paths there were pretty well filled with women, both guests and employees. There were also several others walking along the road going toward the garden.

"Look at all the women that are out," said Paul. "We're going to have a big storm. Real soon."

"What gives you that idea?" said one of the men.

"Why," said Paul, "didn't you know that when a lot of women turn out together like this that it's a sure sign of a storm?"

The guest gazed at the perfectly clear sky, and remarked, "I guess we are safe this time. It doesn't look to me as though there will be a storm for several days at least."

But Paul insisted, "It will rain tomorrow, sure." And true to his prophesy the next morning it was pouring rain from a leaden sky.

When the guest met Paul that morning, he said, "Well, Mr. Smith, you are certainly a good weather prophet. And after this, whenever I see a crowd of women out I shall remember what you said, and shall look for rain." And the two men had a good laugh over the incident.

Drown or Be Shot

C. A. McArthur was the proprietor at McCollom's Hotel in the late 1800s. He was, of course, acquainted with Paul Smith, and he had a story which he liked to tell about Paul.

In the fall of one of those early years Paul and O. D. Seavey, who was connected in some way with the Hotel Champlain, went to McCollom's for a few days of hunting. McArthur served as guide for them and took them one day to Rice Pond, which was not far from the hotel.

McArthur and Mr. Seavey went across the pond in a boat to watch and hunt for deer, while Paul went in another boat in a different direction.

It wasn't long before a deer stepped out in sight of Seavey, and he began shooting, and eventually shot quite a number of times. At first Paul started across the water toward the others, but somehow or other, before he had gone far, he managed to tip the boat over and himself along with it. He went down out of sight, but soon came up and pushed the boat along until he got into shallower water. When he could touch bottom comfortably, he stood there for some time, hanging onto the boat, with only his head and shoulders above water.

McArthur and Seavey had seen the accident happen and, when Seavey had stopped his shooting, they went across the water to see what they could do for Paul. And they asked him how the accident happened.

Of course, Paul wasn't going to admit to any "accident," so he said, 'Happen? I jumped out! On purpose! The bullets were flying around so fast I thought sure I'd be shot! I didn't know which way to go to get out of the way, and I thought I'd be better off under the water than on it. Anyhow I'd rather drown than be shot." And so he turned the laugh away from himself and onto them.

Pick Someone Else's Pocket

During the years that young Paul Smith was working the canal boats from Lake Champlain down to New York City he had become accustomed to spending a few days at a time in the city. He seemed rather to enjoy the business of the city. But the love of the northern area, that he called home, was always there as a strong cord to pull him back before he had been away long.

At some time during those early visits to New York, Paul became familiar with the theater, attending whenever he could.

Paul had a good sturdy, well-built figure. And though he did enjoy fun, and jokes, and joking, he carried himself in a way that gave him the look and manner of an aristocrat. And why should he not look so, after all was he not the head of one of the "first families" of the North Country?

Perhaps — and almost certainly — in the early years, Paul's clothing was of the homespun variety. His pants and coats were very likely to have been cut and made at home. But as time went on, and money became a bit more plentiful to him, Paul was able and did dress "with the best" when occasion demanded it.

Therefore, one need not be surprised that on one of his visits to New York City during his hotel-keeping years that the following event occurred.

As usual Paul went to the theater, and, at least one evening, he had a seat in a theater box. He was always interested in the play, and was attentively watching and listening to all that was happening on the stage when suddenly he realized that something was moving in his pocket. Reaching quickly to investigate, he found himself grasping the right wrist of a very gentlemanly-looking man who was occupying the next seat. His hand was still in Paul's pocket.

Paul slowly drew the hand out of his pocket, and, still keeping a firm hold of the wrist, he said, very quietly, "You're foolish to try that game on me. I was in that game once myself — for fifteen years — down in New Orleans." And he let go of the wrist he held.

The pick-pocket looked much amazed as he listened to Paul's story and it came over him that this man hadn't called for the police; and that his voice was so low and calm that no one around them noticed that anything out of the ordinary was going on. However, when he felt his wrist released with Paul's last word, he didn't hang around to see if this queer individual would change his mind, but lost no time disappearing down an aisle.

Problems to Solve

Many problems arose at Paul Smith's during those early years, and the way they were worked out often made a story that Paul might later use to entertain his guests. The very fact of that period of time, or age, was often part of the problem. The location of the hotel, so far away from a large community, or the railroad, added to it, especially so when there was a death.

If one of the area residents died, the neighbors would come in to help, and they would prepare the body for burial. Embalming was not yet required in this North Country. If they wanted an undertaker, or a casket, they had to send to Plattsburgh or Malone which took several days. (In the last quarter of the 1800s there was a man in Vermontville who served as an undertaker, and he and his wife made caskets; he doing the carpentry work, and she the upholstering.)

If one of the hotel guests died, the hotel carpenter would build a rough box to ship the body home in, unless the person's family ordered a coffin, and then there might be a wait of several days for it to arrive.

"One fall," Paul said, "we had got just about ready to close the big house when some of the fellows brought in a man that had been staying in a camp back in the woods, and he had accidentally shot himself. When they got him as far as my place he wasn't able to go any farther, so we had to keep him here."

"We could all see from the first that he couldn't possibly live very long. So his friends sent for a casket to send him home in after he was dead. He hung onto life and lingered on a few days longer than it had seemed as though he could. And the casket got here several days before he needed it. So that was once that the coffin was waiting for the man instead of the other way around."

He's Not Complainin'

"One year," Paul would say, "a man died here and his friends back in the city wanted his body to reach them at a certain time or it would be too late for the funeral they had planned. I suppose it seemed like plenty of time to them, but it gave us a pretty short time to get him to the train that we would have to send him on. But we said we would do the best we could."

"Some of the men made a rough box to put him in, and it wasn't long before one of my drivers, by the name of Brink, had started to the Ausable Forks station more than 40 miles away. The rough box and its contents was loaded onto one of our 'station wagons,' and the team to haul it was one of our best. Brink knew his team, and he knew he had to make use of every minute if he was to make the specified train. So wherever the road was favorable he 'spanked her right along.' When he got close to Black Brook he stopped at a good place to water his horses. A man that Brink had passed a little farther back on the plank road drove up in his light carriage."

"As he set there a few minutes waiting for the horses to drink he gave a quick look over Brink's load and then he said, 'What you got on there? Is there a dead body in that box?'"

"'Yep,' answered Brink. 'It's the man that died last night.'"

"'Why!' the man sort of gasped, 'when you passed me on the hill back there that box was rattling so it sounded like there was some boards loose. It seems like kind of a rough way to carry a dead person.'"

"Brink gave a quick look around to make sure the box was in place and riding all right. Then he pulled up on the lines a bit, gave a quick signal to the horses, and with a slight grin said to the stranger, 'Well, sir, if the man that's riding in that box back there don't find any fault I don't see as you got any need to.' And off they went at a brisk trot."

"Oh, yes, they got to the station with just a few minutes to spare."

Poor Dog

A sewing machine agent stopped overnight at Paul's one summer, and in the course of a conversation during the evening, he said, "You know when I first began to travel up through here, I never would stop at a log house, for I thought the people who lived in log houses had no money. But I've found out since that some of the people around here who live in log houses have more money than some of those who live in a nice frame house."

In making a reply to that, Paul said, "Up here you can't judge people's pocketbooks by the houses they live in. If you want to know," he went on, "how much money they have, count their dogs. If a man keeps one dog, he's rich. If he has two dogs, he's poor; and if he keeps three dogs, or more, he's damned poor."

What Can You Raise There?

Paul Smith had a great fondness for good horses, and for horse racing. And whenever it was possible he used to go to Burlington, Vermont, at fair time, to take in the horse races. Those visits to the fair also gave Paul a chance to keep in touch with many friends whom he had known since his boyhood days in Milton, Vermont.

One year at the fair he met such a friend who was a farmer. After the hand-shakings and greetings were over, Paul said, half-jokingly, "You'd better go over to the Adirondacks with me, and do your farming over there where you can get much better prices for your produce than you can get here in Vermont."

"What? Go farming in that rough, frosty country?" the Vermonter answered. "Over there where you have nine months of winter, and three months of very late fall; and where the soil is so poor you can't raise a decent crop of anything!"

"They raise more over there than you think they do," said Paul.

"What *do* they raise?" asked the farmer.

"Well," said Paul, "they raise as good vegetables as they do in Vermont, if not better, with the exception of corn and pumpkins. They raise good oats, good rye and buckwheat; plenty of blueberries and lots of good-looking girls and boys. And sometimes, on Town Meeting day, they get drunk and raise the devil," he finished with a laugh.

Rapid Growth

One summer a young man who was not very familiar with the ways of the wilderness, nor of agriculture, arrived at Paul's. He had been there for a few days the summer before, and he seemed to be having a hard time making everything match his year-old memories of the place.

In the early evening, after supper, the young guest was sitting on the piazza, looking earnestly and thoughtfully all around. After awhile, when Paul happened by, the young man stopped him and remarked, "I don't seem to remember those trees being out there last year," and he pointed to a grove of pine trees, each of which was at least 100 feet tall, and large on the stump accordingly. "Were they there last year?" he asked.

"Oh, no!" Paul replied. "They certainly were *not*. We set those trees out there just this past spring." And the questioner sat back in his chair, completely satisfied with the answer, as if he would say, 'I knew I couldn't be mistaken.'"

Black Flies

Two or three guests arrived at Paul Smith's for the first time in the height of the black fly season. After being around the place for a while, with the flies bothering them at every turn, they ran across Paul, and one of the guests remarked, "I should think, Mr. Smith, that those flies must be pretty troublesome in the swamps around here."

Looking and acting astonished, Paul exclaimed, "Flies? Flies? Why, there's no flies in this part of the country."

After watching Paul very closely for a minute or two, one of the men said, "I can't understand it, Mr. Smith. Why is it that the flies don't seem to be bothering you at all? They are just about eating me up."

"Oh! *Those* flies!" Paul replied. "Why, they don't bother *me now* because they know I belong here, and they can get at me at any time. They *always* take the outsiders first."

CHAPTER XIII

Entertainment

Golf Fun

In the course of time the St. Regis Golf Club was formed and a golf course planned and made, near the shores of Osgood Lake. It being about two miles from Paul's hotel, most of the golfers chose to ride rather than walk that distance. Of course they hired their transporation from the hotel. The need for so many to be transported to the same place, at approximately the same time, gave Paul an idea.

He soon either bought, or had especially made, a wagon that would hold 20 people. This he called the "golf wagon," as it was used almost entirely to transport those interested in the game of golf to and from the links. Each person who rode on it paid a set fare, and the project made good business for the horses which Paul kept.

One August morning the golf wagon was pulled up in front of the main entrance of the hotel, and the golfers, both men and women, were on hand with their paraphernalia.

Paul had come down to the steps and was watching the people as they climbed on board and got themselves and possessions settled. Soon there came a merry twinkle in his eyes, and he turned to Frank D. Griswold of New York, who stood near him, and said, "I told the boys," meaning Phelps and Paul, Jr., "to put their golf links right in front of the hotel. But, no, they had to put 'em over there on Osgood Lake and the only way to get to 'em is in a wagon."

"But say," he went on in a lower tone as he stepped over to the side of one of the horses, "the horses look pretty good for having earned $2500 on the golf stage this summer. They've worked hard, and made some money. But they don't know it. I guess they'll stand it." And he grinned with satisfaction.

141

The Malone Fair

Paul Smith nearly always managed to get to the Franklin County Fair which was held at Malone during the early fall of each year. He usually put up at the Flanagan brothers hotel, "The Howard House," in the village. One fair time Paul and Ferd Chase, who was the owner-manager of the Loon Lake House in Loon Lake, had each registered at the hotel. Paul was always a favorite, for everyone that knew him loved to hear his stories and his jokes. They also liked to joke with him, for Paul was just as good-natured about a joke on himself as he was if he could get a joke on someone else. If Chase was around, he would usually play a close second in whatever Paul started. So the two of them were in the midst of a jovial crowd that evening.

Paul Smith loved jewels and after he became financially able, he allowed himself to indulge in the luxury somewhat, and that evening he was wearing a horseshoe-shaped tie pin which was set with diamonds. As one of the Flanagan brothers noticed the pin, he said, "It's no wonder that you hotel men from the South Woods can wear diamonds. You get so much money from all the city people you coax up to your place by telling 'em what a healthy place you've got in the Adirondacks. You praise up the place until they think if they are half, or even two-thirds dead, they'll get well again if they'll only come and stay a spell. Then after they spend most of the summer, and you've got all their money, you tell 'em you're sorry but it looks like they aren't getting much better, so maybe they'd be happier to go back home and die among their friends."

"That's right!" replied Paul with a wink at Chase. "And when we come down here to take in the fair in the fall we have to be right on our toes if we expect to keep all these hungry Malone hotel-keepers from taking all that money away from us."

What's A Bet Among Friends?

The year of 1888 was a presidential election year. Grover Cleveland, a Democrat who was then President, was trying for his second term, while Benjamin Harrison, a Republican, was running against him. Of course, wherever men got together there was much discussion about the candidates, their abilities, qualifications, etc.

Grover Cleveland had been a guest at Paul Smith's hotel several times through the years. In fact, so near as can be determined now, he came there first during the Civil War years, after hiring a substitute to serve in the war in his place.

Though hiring a substitute was a legitimate procedure, it was not considered a very patriotic thing to do; and in later years there were those among his political enemies who used that fact to try to prove that Cleveland was not patriotic, so was not fit for *any* public office, much less the presidency of the country. And it was given out that he went to Paul Smith's to "hide out," supposedly because of his cowardice. At first hearing it may seem that the statement might be true, and that he was indeed very unpatriotic. But the truth of the matter was his two brothers were already in the service, and if Grover went in it would leave their mother and two sisters without anyone to support or care for them; so, it may have been a feeling of duty and love, rather than cowardice that kept him at home.

Anyhow, Cleveland and Paul Smith had already become acquainted, and were fast friends. So, when a guest mentioned in Paul's hearing, that he thought Harrison would be the next President, Paul very promptly said, "I'll bet you an even hundred dollars that Cleveland wins."

The guest replied, "Well, Mr. Smith, I'm not a betting man, but I should think you would be able to find a great many that would take you up on a bet like that."

Paul replied, "I *am* finding some. I'm making all the bets I can on Cleveland. I believe in him."

Time went on. The great day came, and when the votes were all in, Harrison had won and Cleveland has lost that election. As a result Paul lost all his bets which it was rumored ran into the thousands of dollars. No one knew just how much, for he never told, but he paid off every bet without a word of complaint.

Morgan's Ball

Paul Smith came along to the group on the porch, and seeing his favorite chair was empty, he settled down into it and soon asked, "Did I ever tell you about Morgan's ball?" Receiving a negative reply, he settled down into the chair a little more comfortably and started in at his favorite occupation of story-telling.

"There was a feller by the name of Morgan that used to come up here from New York City. He owned large interests in some steamship lines. I s'pose he had "money to burn" as they say, but so far as I know he never tried any of those coin-skipping and cigar-lighting stunts with any of it. He'd give some of it away sometimes if he thought someone needed it. And he never minded using any amount of it if it could buy a little sport or amusement. If there'd been a few dozen men like him up here to throw their money around as he did, there'd have been a plentiful amount of business."

"He came up here to the mountains several times. Once he stayed at Wardner's Hotel at Rainbow Lake. And after that he began coming over here to my place."

"Morgan was the first to put up a real nice camp in the Adirondack Mountains. He had Elverdo Patterson as his head guide, and he really thought a lot of him. They were good friends, as was true in those days of the most of the men and their guides."

"Morgan spent all the time he could, both summer and winter, up here in the mountains. He was always wanting to do something new and different. One night when he got off the train at Ausable Forks on his way up from New York and begged the stage coach driver to let him drive the six-horse team from there to Bloomingdale. It's quite a trick to drive a six-horse team, but he did it without any big trouble. He was so pleased that he gave the driver $15.00 for letting him drive."

"Morgan was a likeable fellow and fairly young. In spite of that, and in spite of his money, there came a day when his doctor had to tell him he had comsumption. I guess that verdict makes a person feel sort of in a hurry to do a lot of living in a short time, and the most of 'em just don't know how to do it."

"Morgan had already done just about everything he could think of that it seemed there was any interest in, except he still wasn't married. So he thought he ought to try matrimony. At least it would be a new experience. So he looked around among his friends and acquaintances until he found a likeable girl who was willing to marry him. In due time they had their wedding in New York City, and they took the first train out for Ausable Forks, and from there they came up to my place by sleigh."

"Morgan had made arrangements with us ahead of time for them to stay here. He had also asked us to plan for a big ball, and he told us to invite everybody for miles around the hotel to come to it. He had us put up notices in different places inviting whole families, fathers, mothers, children, and he said even the cats and dogs were welcome. And he wanted to let everyone know it was all to be free. He even remembered to ask us to be sure to have all the roads plowed out so everyone would have an easier time getting here. All this big spread Morgan was planning in honor of his bride."

"It was New York's Eve, or New Year's Night, of either 1877 or 1878, I can't rightly remember which. But everything was all ready to swing shortly after the newlyweds got here. And the people came. You can just bet they did! There was so many of 'em it seemed if there was anybody in the northern Adirondacks that didn't come they must have been sick-a-bed, or had sore feet."

"When the musicians tuned up for the first dance Morgan was right there with his bride to lead 'em off, and everybody else joined in. He had introduced his wife around, and after that first dance she was kept pretty busy, for she was young and good looking, and a good sport, else she wouldn't have married him in the first place."

"It was right after that first dance that Morgan came to me and said, 'Paul, there's some pretty good looking girls here, and I'm going to dance with every one of 'em.' But he soon discovered the night wouldn't be long enough for that. When he found that out, he just split up the dances and danced with as many as he could. He didn't care if they were the wives, or daughters, of business men, hotel men, merchants, guides, lumbermen, farmers, or day laborers — for they were all here — it was all the same to him. He showed as much honor and courtesy to one as to another."

"Morgan had ordered a big midnight supper for everyone. He had agreed to pay us $5.00 a couple, and they all ate, big and little, young and old, rich and poor."

"He'd had us make a whole barrel-full of lemonade for the ladies and children, and for anyone else who didn't want anything stronger. For those that didn't want lemonade there were drinks to suit all kinds of tastes, and quite a variety of good cigars for smoking. I heard of one young feller from Harrietstown that drank so much champagne that he was sick in bed for several days. I reckon it was the first champagne he ever drank, and apparently it was also the last for they said the first thing he did as soon as he was able to sit up in bed and use his right hand was to sign a temperence pledge. And I hear he has stuck to it ever since."

"You know if that fellow, Morgan, had held a few more such balls at my hotel, I'd soon have been richer than Rockefeller."

"Morgan danced steadily all night except for the short time that he took out for supper, and for an occasional drink. When he got too warm he took off his coat and vest, rolled his shirt sleeves up to his elbows and danced on. The most of the men was doing just about the same. They came for a good time and they were all doing their best to have it."

"The ball was still going strong when daylight came, and they quit soon after that. As the party broke up you could hear folks all around you saying they had had the best time of their lives. But I feel pretty sure Morgan, himself, had the best time of all. And his bride run him a close second.

"But," continued Paul, "time went on, and all too soon Morgan was nearing the end of his life. And one spring day when he was back in New York, he was down pretty low. He knew he couldn't push himself much farther. He wasn't able to come to the Adirondacks, so he sent for his guide and friend to come to him. Patterson reached him a short time before Morgan passed on. When Morgan's will was read Patterson found he had not been forgotten."

Thoughtful Dancers

For some years before the dance hall was built at Paul's a large tent was set up to be used for dancing.

One night one of the male guests gave a ball for the hotel guests and their friends. When they had all danced as long as they cared to, the host told the guides that they and the rest of the help could finish out the evening and the refreshments, and, that the musicians would continue to play for them as long as they liked.

Of course the guides and the help were glad to accept that treat, and they were soon gathered at the tent and the dance went on. Some time later Mrs. Smith sent word to the musicians to stop playing, as she felt her "girls" needed to get to bed and rest for the day's work that was ahead. That stopped the most of the dancing, but there were some who continued to dance without the music. They were far from being quiet, and it wasn't long before Paul went in, and in his quiet off-hand way, said, "All right, boys. Put the lights out, and call it enough. You're making so much noise it disturbs the guests. We can hear you all over the plce."

That was all that was needed. The lights went out promptly, and the place was soon quiet for the night.

Trips with Friends

Charles H. Bennett, of Racquette Lake, was a friend of Paul Smith for many years. The two men often took short trips together.

Bennett always enjoyed Paul's wit, and used to say that he never knew anyone to get the better of Paul, though a great many had tried, as he had himself.

One winter the two men went together to the Saranac Lake carnival. The village was crowded with visitors. The first night Bennett got a room at one end of the town, and Paul's room was at the further end.

The second day they managed to find a room at the Riverside Inn where they could both stay. They would have to sleep together, but they didn't mind that.

As they were preparing for bed that night they got to talking about other times, and conditions they had each faced in the hotel business and of their own problems and struggles.

Bennett finally said, "I wasn't as fortunate as you were. I ran away from home when I was still a boy, and built a camp on Racquette Lake. I hunted deer, and sold them in the market for a dollar. I carried logs on my back for five years before I ever got fifty cents saved."

Paul didn't make any response to Charles' outburst, so Bennett continued, emphatically. "You know Paul, I never had $50,000 given me to start with. I had to . . . ."

Paul interrupted by saying, "Now, go on, Charley! You make me hungry. My wife and I slept in a clothes basket for five years."

Bennett had nothing more to say on the subject. Nor did he ever again try to compare his lot with Paul Smith's.

CHAPTER XIV

Serious Changes Come

By the spring of 1890 Paul and Lydia Smith had been married 31 years. It had been a prosperous period of time for them. During those years they had acquired nearly 20,000 acres of land, much of it adjoining the hotel property. They bought 6,000 acres in 1887 from the Mutual Life Insurance Company, 4,000 acres from Harriet Vilas, and another 4,000 acre tract from the Ducy and Backus Lumber Company in 1889. Be it understood that many of the acres of property which Paul and Lydia owned were not land, but water, and in the course of time they owned the whole of ten lakes and ponds, and portions of a number of others — both the Lower and Upper St. Regis Lakes, Spitfire Lake and Osgood Pond were among them. Also, the Saranac River and many smaller streams ran across or bordered some of their land.

Paul Smith was 65 years old in August of 1890, and apparently it gave him a feeling that he was "getting along in years" and that he had better be making plans for someone else to have the authority, and the ability to carry on his various businesses when the time came that he could no longer do so. Anyhow, be that as it may, on December 12, 1890, Paul called his family together and the "Paul Smith's Hotel Company" was organized. The Company's directors for the first year were Apollos A. Smith, Sr., Lydia H. Smith, Henry B. L. Smith, Phelps Smith, Apollos A. Smith, Jr.; with Paul Sr. serving as president.

Illness and Death

During the last few years Lydia had been troubled by a persistent cough, which had been especially bothersome in the winter time. So for a year or two Paul had taken Lydia to Florida for a portion of the winter in the hope that the warmer climate would bring relief from the cough. Therefore, it so happened that very early in January of 1891, Paul and Lydia were on their way to

149

Florida, presumably by train. Somewhere along the way the word reached them that their son Henry had died on January 3rd. His illness had been diagnosed as pneumonia, which in those days was a very serious, and far too often, a very brief and fatal, disease.

In a state of shock the travelers turned back home to attend to the burial of this, their eldest son, whose life had ended so suddenly, before he was 30 years of age. Henry's death struck them both very hard, and his mother could not seem to rise above it. In spite of the fact that she and Paul were so very close, she apparently grieved herself to death, for she died in the fall of that same year.

With wife, mother and eldest son gone, life could never be the same for the Smith men. In spite of their own sorrow, the "boys," Phelps, 29, and Paul, Jr., 20 did all they could to comfort and strengthen their father. But, Paul was so tired and burdened with grief that he felt he had to get away for awhile. The Hotel Company would carry on. At his own request, Paul, Sr. was put on a salary, while the actual on-the-job management of the hotel and its sidelines was turned over to Phelps and Paul, Jr., as the remaining members of the company. This arrangement left Paul, Sr. free to get away from the place if he so desired, and he could be sure that everything was being taken care of as he had planned.

A Man Should Leave His Mark

Perhaps the death of his wife and son left a more terrible emptiness in Paul than people would have thought. It has been said that the place where a man has passed should show some evidence of how he lived while there. Certainly one would not have to look closely, nor far, to find evidence of how Paul Smith lived while in the Adirondacks. His trail was left plain enough so that "he who ran could read" and that trail still shows.

When Paul Smith entered the Adirondacks as a hunter, he and the area were both practically unknown to the world at large. More than 60 years later, when he answered the call to Eternity's far shore, both he and the area in which he had lived were known the world around, because of the trails he had made. When he came to the Adirondacks in 1848 and opened up his first hunting camp on rented property, he was absolutely inexperienced and unknown in the realm of hotel keepers.

Yet, from the very first there were well-known and noted men of the world who stopped for awhile at Paul's hotel. Besides those already mentioned were Peter Butler of Boston, and Horace Green of New York, who were some of the first to arrive shortly after the new hotel was opened in 1859.

Others to come later for short or longer periods of time were President Benjamin Harrison, President Teddy Roosevelt, Alfred E. Smith, Robert Louis Stevenson, E. H. Harriman, Rockefeller, W. Seward Webb, Ex-Governor Levi P. Morton, and many, many others.

"Camps" Spring Up

Paul had not been at St. Regis long before he had the foresight to see that Adirondack land which contained lakes, ponds, and streams was going to be in great demand in the future. Thereafter, he bought property whenever opportunity offered if he could manage the finances. Paul sold small lots to a number of his friends and guests who wanted to be near the hotel and have a part in the social life, yet be in their own homes. Dr. H. B. Loomis, of New York City, who had loaned Paul the money for the building of the hotel on the St. Regis shore, was among the first to buy a building lot. The land which he chose was about an acre in size on the lake shore, and it included an elevation of ground on which he built a cottage which soon became known as the Loomis Cottage. There came the time years later in 1890 when the doctor decided to dispose of the property, and Paul and Lydia bought it back from him.

Much of the building material, such as boards, shingles, timbers, blinds, doors and windows had been sawed out and made in Paul Smith's mills from logs harvested from the mature forests owned by himself. Sometimes the very trees that were cut on a site were sawed and worked up into the various types of materials that were to be used in the buildings that were planned for that same site. Paul eventually sold campsites for 100 or more of the "camps" that were built in that immediate area.

Morgan, of Morgan's Ball fame, was said to have been the first to put up a "nice camp" in the Adirondacks. Young Hoffman, who was the son of Dean Hoffman of Brooklyn, New York, built his camp, which he called Camp Hoff, across the lake from the hotel. His whole camp was brightly illuminated, the lighting being so placed that a part of the lights formed a huge red and white cross which shone out very effectively, each evening, against the dark background of the forest.

Whenever he was staying at his camp "young Hoffman" served

as usher in the "tiny Episcopal Church," always seating the people and taking up the offerings. It used to be said that if he ever heard the "vulgar rattle of a coin" as it dropped into the plate that it made him so sick that he had to go at once and take "sal volatile," for it was such a change from the "modest s-s-ish" of the five dollar bill to which he was accustomed.

Dr. Edward Trudeau built a camp in a beautiful spot on Spitfire Lake, to which he and his family came often for many years. As the doctor became more and more well-known as a specialist in "lung troubles," so the Adirondacks became known and visited as a natural health resort.

By the year of 1890 there were more than 100 camps, or summer homes, many of them very elaborate, almost palatial buildings, within a radius of three miles from Paul's hotel. Land that bordered the shores of the St. Regis Lakes, Spitfire, Osgood and such was priced from $2500 to $10,000 an acre. Some of the homes that were built on such lots as those cost many thousands of dollars, even then when a thousand dollars would buy many times what it will now. Quite a number of smaller, and less costly, camps were built on the Lower St. Regis, a little nearer to the hotel. These were used by their owners mainly as day camps, or a place to go for a day, or a weekend of picnicking. Often such camps as those had only three walls with a roof and a floor.

Through the years that have passed many of the "camps" have been sold and resold, and because of that their names have also been changed a time or two, so it would be hard to name all the original owners today. But among them were the Garretts, Frederick W. Vanderbilt, the Honorable Whitelaw Reid, Anson Phelps Stokes, Gould, Pratt, George Dodge and the Lymans. H. McKay Twombly paid $5,000 for the rental of one camp for one summer. Col. Payne paid $1,500 for one acre of land on which to build a cottage for his nephews and nieces.

Irving Berlin had a cottage built, which at some time later on had to be removed "because it obstructed the operation of automobiles." But, during the months that Berlin occupied the cottage he made such good use of the telephone and the telegraph wires, usually between the hours of midnight and 3:00 A.M., that he was able to woo and win Miss MacKay, the young lady who later became his wife. Miss MacKay was the daughter of Clarence MacKay who was at that time president and principal owner of the Postal Telegraph and Cable Company.

There came the time during the last quarter of the 19th century that the shores of the Upper St. Regis Lake were so thickly populated that there was not a foot of land for sale. And every man who had bought and built there was at least a millionaire — some of them ten times over. Someone at that time remarked, "If there's a spot on the face of the earth where millionaires go to play at housekeeping in log cabins and tents as they do right here, I have yet to hear about it." Someone also remarked back in those "good old days" that Paul Smith's was "one of the very few places in this country where nobody locks a door or a trunk, but where nothing has ever been stolen."

Besides the millionaires who built their own elaborate "camps" on the St. Regis Lakes there were those not so rich who wanted to have a summer home in the area. So the Smiths built a number of attractive cottages which they rented or leased for a year or more at a time. Some of those buildings were built to the size and design that the renter desired, and requested. Others were designed by the Smiths. Each so-called cottage was beautiful and added much to the charm of the particular place in which it was setting. Each of these cottages, as well as those mentioned above bore the name of the occupant such as The Harriman, Hill, Glover, Baker, Walker, Kellogg, MacAlpin, Turner, Millbank, Fletcher, Moffatt, Lambert, McNaughton, Whitney and so on.

Growing Bigger

During the years between 1890 and 1905 the growth of Paul's place was really remarkable. Paul and his sons, Phelps and Paul, Jr., greatly enlarged the hotel itself. They built a connecting annex, a beautiful new store and an office with living quarters on the second floor which were used as a home by the Smith men. They put up a large stable in which 50 to 60 horses were kept; also a blacksmith shop; a wood-working shop; an electrical shop; a large dormitory for women; and another for the men. They also built a four-story warehouse; a saw mill; a planing mill; two boiler houses; a large launch house; a laundry building; a large woodshed; a beautiful casino building which was located on the shore of Lower St. Regis Lake. That building housed a stock exchange with a direct wire to the Stock Exchange in New York City; a bowling alley; pool room; grill room and kitchen. There were also sleeping quarters on the third floor and boat lockers and launch slips on the ground floor. To go along with the new stock-exchange office with its line to the Stock Exchange in New York, Paul established his own "Paul Smith's Telegraph Company" with new and modern wiring and fixtures. Sometime a little later Paul established his own telephone company which served not only his hotel and other buildings, but the surrounding camps, and neighborhood as well. Many of the guests who came to the hotel and to the nearby camps and cottages felt the need of keeping a "finger on the pulse" of their homes and businesses even though they were vacationing, so they made good use of the wires.

There was a saw mill on the St. Regis River that crossed the property that Paul had bought at Keese's Mills. In the course of time the Smiths had that mill converted to an electrical power plant which supplied the great hotel, cottages, and other buildings with power for lights, thus, the candles and kerosene lamps were relegated to the past. Eventually they extended these electric lines to reach and supply many of the camps along the lakes with lights and power.

During all its early years the hotel had lacked modern conveniences, and the Hotel Company almost seemed to pride itself in that fact. But during those years just before and after the turn of the century great changes were made along that line. The little matter of piping water into the hotel was among the first of the modern conveniences to become a reality; and of course with the water flowing, modern bathrooms, with modern plumbing soon followed. After that just about anything that could be thought of that would make work easier, or life more pleasant was added to the establishment and put into service.

The Hotel Company established an express office in the hotel and took care of all express packages for the hotel and camps, and cashed all checks. They also employed a hotel lawyer, and a physician, and kept a drug store.

They launched pleasure boats on the lakes which were run with storage batteries that were kept charged with electricity from their own power plant. Just about everything that could be thought of to amuse the guests was made available, such as golf, baseball, tennis, canoeing, sailing, yachting with weekly yacht races which hundreds of people gathered to watch. There was bathing, fishing, hunting, driving, riding and the like. There were also pool and bowling, an occasional dance and other amusements for indoors.

Paul tried his best to have anything and everything on hand that anyone might need or want. In fact, if you wanted to send a letter, telegram, or express package you were advised to "go to Paul." If you needed lumber to build a house, canvas for a tent, meat for dinner, a boat or a horse and carriage, "go to Paul." If you desired a complete outfit for rough camping, a guide for a day, week or for the season, the latest novel or a postage stamp, you would "go to Paul."

According to one little story that has come down to us, Paul did his best to have the best quality of everything to be had, even to cold weather. It seems that February 1904 had some extremely cold nights and one morning when the men who made up the winter family at the hotel were talking about it, word came through that it was -40°, -42°, and -48° below at Lake Placid, Saranac Lake and Bloomingdale respectively.

Paul had listened silently to all that was said. When the reports were all in the men were agreed that it could be no colder anywhere. Then Paul spoke up and said that it was -52° below at the hotel. To prove it he went on to say, "It was so cold that the nail the thermometer hung on froze off close to the building and it dropped to the ground. But that didn't do any harm as the thermometer was frozen so hard to the clapboards that it couldn't drop." One of the old St. Regis guides who was present began to laugh and to crow, and said, "Old Paul fooled 'em bad! He certainly skinned 'em all that time!"

Another Deal Goes Through

In Paul Smith's looking around to "see what he could see" there came the day soon after the 1900s came in when he decided that the power at Franklin Falls had greater possibilities than just to run a small lumber mill. There was also a second mill at Union Falls, just a few miles down the river from Franklin Falls. Although he was nearing 78 years of age, Paul decided that he must have those properties if he could manage it. So he bagan to make inquiries as much as he could without giving anyone an idea that he was interested. He hadn't told his sons, Phelps and Paul, what he had in mind and had his plans pretty well worked out for buying the two properties when they discovered what he was up to. They were really alarmed, because it seemed to them like a very foolish move, and unnecessary expense; and they hurriedly sent for P. T. Hanscom of the General Electric Company who had helped and advised them with the setting up of the Keese's Mills Plant some years before.

Mr. Hanscom came promptly and went with the boys to look over the two sites, and the area that would be involved. After careful inspection he assured the "boys" that their father was *not* "crazy;" but that those two sites were very worthwhile, valuable spots to buy and develop.

So Paul's projected deal went through and when the purchase of the mills was accomplished the boys helped their father in the business connected with the acquiring of all the lands that would be flooded if, and when, dams were built across the Saranac River at each of these points.

The work of installing electrical power plants at Franklin Falls and Union Falls started in 1904-1905. Dams had to be constructed across the Saranac River above the sites of the projected power houses. Land, much land, had to be searched out, lines surveyed, titles searched and land bought for several miles up and down each side of the river, for the water that would be held back above the dams had to have room to spread out to make the ponds or lakes that would be formed by the held-back water.

Transmission lines had to be run from the power plants that had yet to be built at each of the two sites, to Bloomingdale, then on to Paul Smiths and surrounding areas.

At some time during those two years when all that work was going on, the Smith men organized the Paul Smith Electric Light and Power Company. Paul, Sr. was put in as president of this company also, with his two sons making up most of the company. It was not long after that that the Smiths bought the Saranac Lake Light, Heat and Power Company and combined it with their own original company and name, and were soon supplying electricity 40 miles in one direction and 30 miles in another.

CHAPTER XV

The Fruits of Labor

The years came and passed, but for all his increasing age Paul Smith seemed as well and strong in body, and as alert and keen in mind as ever. It seemed that he was always looking for some way to improve the area in which he lived. He seemed to think of the northern Adirondacks as his own back yard, and was ever trying to make some changes to better it.

In the beginning, he could only take into account the points he was able to reach as he traveled about on foot, along partially hidden paths that led off in various directions. As he acquired horses he was able to broaden his range of inspection considerably.

He owned fine riding horses for his own convenience and enjoyment as well as for his guests; and, thereafter, when time allowed, he spent many hours each week in the saddle. It was sometimes said of him, even after he was well past 70 year of age, that "Paul Smith sits his horse like a centaur."

But, in the course of time, the day came when Paul decided he could rest somewhat from his labor and see the world outside his Adirondack home.

He visited every important city in the United States, and in Canada. He also went on several different moose hunting trips into Canada, and according to his life-time friend, Lem Merrill, when on one of those hunting trips in 1903 he became interested in a "cobalt silver" mine. And Merrill went on to say that the deposit of cobalt silver was discovered accidentally when a black-smith by the name of LaRose threw a heavy hammer at a red fox. The hammer missed the fox but hit the cliff beyond it, and broke off a chunk of rock from the face of the cliff. This revealed a four-inch vein of silver that gleamed when wet. When samples of the ore were assayed it was found to have a 90 percent content of silver. Thirty-seven claims of 40 acres each were staked out, and a mining company was formed with Paul Smith as president and Lem

Merrill as secretary. The company was given the name of "The Gogandia Silver Mine" (Gogandia is an Indian word meaning giant). Lem did the surveying for the company. (No reference as to the working of the mine, or of its yield has been found by this writer.)

Even as a young man working on the canal boats Paul had enjoyed the traveling, and the changes of scenery that constantly met his eye. But as a husband and father, and the proprietor of a popular hotel, there had not been much time for travel except for an occasional business trip. As time went on Phelps and Paul, Jr. took over more and more of the responsibilities connected with the management of the hotel and the various other businesses. Paul, Sr. still retained presidency of the Hotel Company, but with Lydia gone and his sons looking after things so well, he began to take trips here and there until he had traveled over a great deal of the United States, and parts of Canada. But his desires never led him across the ocean.

A man by the name of James M. Bell of New York City came to the Hotel every season for 45 years. During that time he and Paul became close friends and he sometimes accompanied Paul on his travels. One year, the two men went down into Florida and took a boat trip on the Indian River. It was Paul's first trip down the river and he found it a beautiful country. The voyage — if we may call it that — took them about 250 miles through the most fascinating scenery. In some places the river was only 100 feet wide, while in others it was as much as three to six miles in width.

The men were on a paddle-wheel boat, and Paul enjoyed looking over the side of the boat, and down into the depths of the clear water, which was, in some places, as much as 30 feet deep, to watch the fish and other creatures. Sometimes the boat would push its way through a school of silver-sided fish, and the colors, blue, silver, pink and purple which they reflected, were splendid to see.

Paul was charmed with the whole trip, but being Paul he had to get a little fun out of it, so one day he carelessly remarked, "This Injun River is certainly very beautiful."

"It's *Indian* River," Mr. Bell corrected him.

"No, its *Injun*," Paul said. "I guess I should know. We have Injuns in the Adirondacks."

"I tell you it's *I-n-d-i-a-n*," Mr. Bell spelled out to him.

He and Paul were sitting on the upper deck, and without saying anything more Paul left his seat and went below. Soon he was opening a conversation with another passenger, with the comment, "Fine River."

"Yes, suh!" the man said. "A mighty fine rivah."

"Live around here?" Paul asked.

"Yes, suh! Mos' all mah life. Got a place daown heah whar Ah growed up," was the answer.

"What is the name of this river?" Paul asked.

The reply that Paul was hoping for came strong and sure; "Injun Rivah, suh."

"Thank you!" Paul said, and he immediately rose from his seat and lost no time getting back to the upper deck where he had left his friend. He greeted Mr. Bell with, "Say, Jim, there's a fellow down on the lower deck who has lived on this river all his life. Come on down and visit with him," and back Paul went closely followed by Bell.

After introducing the two men, Paul said to the southerner, "You say you've lived here most all of your life. Will you please tell my friend the name of this river."

The stranger promptly replied, "It's Injun Rivah, suh!"

"There you see!" said Paul turning to Bell. "I told you it was *Injun* River, and it ain't *nothing else*." And Paul went off chuckling gleefully to think how he had proved his point.

Although he had little use for education in his younger days, Paul came to have more respect for it as he grew older. For some years he was a great lover of Shakespeare; and he became a tireless reader as the years flew by, always keeping up with the news, and he drew many an object lesson from the things he read. He was never bothered by having to wear glasses, and his hearing always remained good.

As has been said, James Bell often accompanied Paul on his travels, and in discussing Paul's qualities as a traveler he said, "Paul Smith is a remarkable man. He is so modest and unassuming, and is as much at home in southern California as he is in the Adirondacks. Nearly everywhere he goes he meets people he knows. And wherever he goes he makes new friends. Paul is never disturbed, nor upset, but is always perfectly at ease. He is always so full of fun, and wit, that he keeps people sitting on the edge of their seats, wondering what is coming next."

His calmness and composure were rarely, if ever, disturbed. As an illustration of this, Mr. Bell told the following story. "One winter Paul was spending some time at his cottage in California. One afternoon we went to call on some ladies at their cottage at Coronado Beach. Paul was in his very best mood, full of fun, and lively."

"The conversation had turned to Paul's affairs, and to his home in the Adirondacks. Someone had asked if he had a son, and Paul said, 'Yes, I have a son. In fact, I have two sons and neither one of 'em is married.' Then Paul went on and described his sons, and told the ladies that he had tried most awfully hard to get them to marry, but both of them were very indifferent to the idea."

"'Why,' he said, 'I'll give any one of you ladies $5000 in cash if you will plan a match and marry my son, Paulie, off to some good girl. Yes! I'd make it . . .'"

"The offer was never finished," said Mr. Bell, "for at that instant Paul, Jr. stepped out of an automobile, and started to walk up to the cottage veranda. He was all covered up with automobile toggery and you wouldn't expect anyone to recognize him. But Paul had whirled around when he heard the car door open, and recognized the son about whom he had just been talking, and whom he had every reason to believe was across the country in the midst of the Adirondack Mountains."

"Paul certainly was surprised and astonished," said Mr. Bell, "but he didn't show it. With scarcely a halt in the sentence, he continued, 'but here is my little boy, Paulie himself. Look him over and see if the job of marrying him off isn't worth $5000.'"

"Paul, Jr. was the center of attraction for a few minutes and Paul never let on that he hadn't expected his son to appear just when he did."

Wrongly Using a Name

According to a news item which had been clipped from a July, 1906, *Adirondack Enterprise* newspaper, a well-known Tupper Lake wholesale liquor dealer was advertising and selling a brand of whiskey which was called "Paul Smith's Brand." The label on the whiskey bottles bore a copy of Paul Smith's photograph, and of his signature, and the words, "Paul Smith Maryland Rye bottled in bond. Meyer Newman, Baltimore, MD."

The dealer had been selling this brand of whiskey, so labeled, for more than a year. Paul had evidently objected to having his picture and signature used in such a way, but his objections apparently did no good. So Paul took his case to the Malone firm of

Badger and Cantwell who presented it before the Franklin County Supreme Court. They brought action for $1000 damages, and a requirement that Newman should stop using Smith's name, picture and signature on their whiskey bottles. A temporary injunction was issued by Justice Van Kirk at a special term of Supreme Court at Greenwich, restraining Newman from using the labels.

Mr. Smith claimed that Newman was using these labels without his consent, and he feared it would injure his business as the proprietor of a summer resort to have his name and picture so used.

This news clipping goes on to say that "Newman's attorney, U.S. Wade, will fight the action," for he claimed to have permission from Paul to make the labels, which had been quite an expense to him, and it would be a great loss to discontinue their use.

The article closes with these words, "Outcome will be awaited with interest." (But no further reference to the matter has been found by this writer.)

Illness Is Hard to Take

Paul Smith had always been a strong and vigorous man. He had scarcely ever felt ill in his life, and had enjoyed the best of health throughout the years. To be sure he had lived in the out-of-doors almost all his life; a good share of those years was spent in the mountains where he had the benefit of the pure, invigorating air. His way of life surely did much to keep him well. It was fortunate that Paul had enjoyed good health for he hadn't much patience with doctors, and thought there was more "humbug" about them than in the most of the rest of the human race.

But there was one time, during the years when he might have been considered to be past middle-age, that he was taken with a sickness. The nature of his ailment is not now known, but he became very ill for some days.

A doctor was called, and he gave the order that seemed to be the first one given by all physicians back then, "Let me see your tongue." He felt Paul's pulse, left some medicine, and went away, all the time looking wise, but saying very little.

Although the doctor called everyday, Paul got no better, but continued to be very ill. Finally, a messenger was sent to Malone to call a doctor from there. When he came his first command to Paul was also, "Let me see your tongue." He also took the patient's pulse, and looked wise. Then he said, after looking over the medicines on the stand, "I'm going to change your medicine." With that he shoved back the old medicines, measured out the new ones, and almost immediately left the house. Paul was impatient and disgusted, and as soon as he was sure that he was alone in the room he swept up all the medicines within his reach, and sent them flying through the open window. Even then Paul must have been "on the road to recovery," for in just a few days he was able to be around much as usual.

In telling about it afterward Paul would finish his story with, "I got well without their medicines, and I've lived to tell about it a good many times."

Birthdays Come As Birthdays Will

The years kept rolling on and Paul Smith's 77th birthday, August 20, 1902 came along. Some of his friends planned a surprise dinner for him. He received many gifts, and several speeches were given that were carefully planned to express the high esteem and affection which people far and near had for him.

Paul Smith, or "Uncle Paul" as he was then commonly called by the generation younger than his own, was greatly touched by it all. The eyes that were, even at 77, usually twinkling with fun were filled with tears. And when the speeches were finished, and it was his turn to respond, that tongue which was always so quick with an answer faltered, and with quavering voice he said, "How I wish my wife could see this!"

As the years had passed on, Paul Smith had turned over to his sons, Phelps and Paul, Jr., more and more of the responsibilities of running the hotel, and other businesses, which he had started. Eventually he found himself with nothing that required his care. Life with nothing demanding his attention did not seem to suit him, so he set about acquiring a job for himself. All on his own, and to everyone's surprise, he obtained the use of a garage, the location of which is unknown today, bought several automobiles, and set up a car rental business.

Just about every morning after that one could find him out bright and early, "happy as a lark," going about the garage, inspecting the cars to make sure they were clean and ready for the day's business.

Beside the pleasure of meeting and talking with people, he had the satisfaction of seeing the new idea work out. Paul also enjoyed being able to say, "Well! I ain't getting rich, but I'm doing good.

I'm making a little change for my pocket."

As Paul moved on into his 80s he was still "hale and hearty," well-poised and well-balanced; and though a trifle bent, and, of course, slightly lame as a result of the injuries sustained in the fall from a barn some years before, he still carried his tall, broad, big-boned frame in a youthful manner. And he was ever eager and alert.

His favorite dress was a blue serge suit, with a flower in his lapel, his neat Van Dyke beard, snow white hair, the twinkling blue eyes, the suggestion of a smile, his favorite light gray felt, broad-brimmed hat, all served to accentuate his still pleasing personality. Paul Smith still loved people and was nearly always surrounded by friends, whether at home or abroad.

On his 80th birthday Paul was the honored guest at a birthday dinner given for him at the camp of Henry L. Hotchkiss on Spitfire Lake.

Dreams Never Die

If one counted his age by the number of years he had lived, Paul Smith was already an old man when he started a project of which he had dreamed for a number of years. He wanted a branch of the railroad to go closer to the hotel so his guests wouldn't have to be transported so many miles by stage coach.

The hotel that had started out as a hunting camp for men had grown into a full-fledged summer resort for men, women, and children; and for many years was the most popular mountain resort in the whole country. During those years the railroads had crept much closer than they were at first; but Paul, never satisfied with good if better could be had, or with better if best were possible, still dreamed of a time when the railroad would stop at his door.

After the New York Central came as close as Lake Clear Junction, (a matter of about seven miles) one would suppose Paul might have been satisfied to have a station that near. But not Paul. He still dreamed of the possibility of the railroad passing, or possibly ending as his hotel.

Every little while Paul contacted the officials of the New York Central Railroad and tried his best to persuade them to run a line from the Junction to his place, but they wouldn't listen to him. Paul felt they were a little short-sighted, as the fares from his guests alone would bring quite a tidy sum.

One day when the railroad officials brushed him off as usual, without half listening to him, he said, "I've a good notion to build the road myself." That remark brought a derisive laugh from all those present. And they began to make jokes about "Smith's paper railroad."

Paul Smith was old enough to be childish, or senile, for he was near 80, but his mind was as clear, and his thinking as young and daring as ever.

Two or three years later two old men sat in a car on the "paper railroad." No one ever having seen him could fail to know that the tall one with the snow white hair, the laugh-wrinkles in his face, the twinkling blue eyes, the carefully-tailored clothes and the wide-brimmed gray felt hat, was Paul Smith. The other man, who was about the same age, was short and thin, with iron-gray hair. His eyes were deep-set, and gentle beneath heavy eyebrows and he looked somewhat like a lost child. He and Paul had been chums during their youthful days, and the friendship had held all through the years; and he was just leaving to go to his home in a small village in Vermont, after spending a few days with Paul at his hotel.

The two friends were having their last visit as they waited for the time when the train was to start. In that visit Paul was telling his chum about the railroad and about how he had come to build it. One can hardly understand how Paul had left such an important subject for conversation as the last thing to be talked about, but so it came about. (Although we have no way of knowing, it is quite likely that his friend was the Hiram "Harm" Washburn mentioned in Chapter I.)

With a ring of happiness, and of something akin to pride in his voice, Paul said, "Every foot of it is on my own land. When I said, 'I'd a good notion to build it myself,' those New York Central men laughed at the "foolish idea." They said it couldn't be done, and called it a "paper railroad." They said if I paid the surveyors I'd do well. I let 'em laugh. There wasn't much I *could* do about *that*. But I decided right then and there that I *would* do something about the railroad."

"My trunk was all packed to go to California, but I went home and unpacked it; and I started the men to work right *there* on that biggest cut. It took a while; a lot of planning; plenty of hard work; and quite a pile of money."

"When the thing was done, Brown of the Central came down

here, and wanted to ride out on the first trip. 'Pears he'd been watching the railroad get built, and knew just when to come. That first trip was going to be made by a big steam engine, and a heavy car. I didn't get it changed to electric power 'til about a year later. The electricity comes from my Union Falls power house."

"I was scared the whole thing maybe wouldn't go at all, or would go in the ditch, and I tried to persuade Brown not to go on it. But he 'wanted to try the paper railroad,' he said;" and Paul laughed, as he added, "So he went."

"Well," Paul said, "everything worked just as it was supposed to, and, when we reached Lake Clear Junction, Brown took off his hat, and says he, 'Paul, I give up! You've *done* it! And I think you're the only man that ever *would* have done it. But it has cost you a lot of money.'"

"'Well,' says I, 'that's all right! 'T'was my own money, and every foot of that road is on my own land.'" Then with a quick look at his chum, and a boyishly triumphant laugh, he continued, "The New York Central wants to buy it now."

Just then a gong sounded and the two men got to their feet. They clasped hands, and bade each other "Good-bye!" The one old man looked back wistfully as the train carried him along through the Adirondack forest. The other stood on the platform and watched as the train rolled out of sight. Then he made his way slowly and thoughtfully toward the great hotel a few rods distant. That man was Paul Smith — canal boatman, hunter and guide, pioneer hotel proprietor and owner, financier, railroad builder and owner — Paul Smith, still an unspoiled young-old man, whose victories in the Adirondacks will ever be his most enduring monument.

That "paper railroad" of Paul Smith's was built in 1906. And it was in that same year that the words, "and Railroad" were added to the company's name, "Paul Smith's Electric Light and Power and Railroad Company." Although the electric train and railroad that Paul wanted hadn't become a reality yet, Paul was working at it with full determination to complete it, which he did. And when completed it extended from the New York Central Railroad in Lake Clear Junction to Paul Smith's Hotel, in Paul Smith's, New York.

To fulfill completely Paul's dream for the service of his railroad, the officials in charge of other lines were consulted, and between them all it was arranged that those who so desired could obtain a

Pullman reservation in New York City, and go on through without a change to Paul's. The cars could be shifted from train to train without disturbing the passengers. As an extra service, for the guests who might be making a morning arrival by Pullman, a bellboy was on board with the needed "tools" and ingredients to serve hot coffee, or a complete breakfast to any who desired it. In those early days many of the wealthy people owned their own railroad cars. And, after Paul's line was finished, they could get to and from Paul's much more conveniently than before.

At first on Paul's railroad the trains were run by steam-powered engines. About a year later he had the needed lines installed, and the necessary changes made to convert the railroad from steam to an electric railway. The electricity was supplied by Paul's power plant at Union Falls. The electric locomotives had sufficient power to haul the extra cars the same as the steam engines did. The work of changing the railroad to an electric line was completed about the first of June 1908.

Paul's Electric Railway, the so-called "paper railroad," was really only a one-car train; that one car being fitted with modern conveniences for the comfort of its passengers, for carrying baggage and freight, the U.S. Mail, and so on. It also had the power and ability to haul private railroad cars as well as Pullmans from Lake Clear Junction to the Hotel. And, on occasion, was used to haul pulp wood from Paul Smith's to the Junction, hauling up to as many as eight carloads at one trip.

The Electric Railway was Paul's pride and joy for the remainder of his life and for many years thereafter it was of great use to both the hotel and its guests until the hotel burned shortly after Labor Day in 1933.

The following is a time table for Paul's railroad as given in the *Adirondack Enterprise* of August 20, 1908, Paul Smith's 83rd birthday.

PAUL SMITH'S ELECTRIC RAILWAY

Paul Smith's Hotel and the St. Regis Chain of
Lakes Connections at Lake Clear Junction with
passenger trains on the New York Central.
Paul Smith's Hotel to Lake Clear Junction.

	A.M.	A.M.	P.M.	P.M.	P.M.
Lv. Paul Smith's	6:30	11:15	1:30	5:50	8:00
Ar. Lake Clear	6:55	11:45	1:55	6:20	8:30

Lake Clear Jct. to Paul Smith's Hotel

Lv. Lake Clear Jct.	7:10	11:50	2:05	6:30	8.45
Ar. Paul Smith's	7:40	12:20	2:35	7:00	9:15

Lake Placid, Saranac Lake to Paul Smith's Hotel via New York Central

Lv. Lake Placid		10:50	1:15	5:35	7:45
Lv. Saranac Lake	6:35	11:20	1:40	6:00	8:10
Ar. Paul Smith's	7:40	12:20	2:35	7:00	9:15

Paul Smith's Hotel to Saranac Lake and Lake Placid

Lv. Paul Smith's	6:30	11:15	1:25	5:50	8:00
Ar. Saranac Lake	7:40	12:15	2:40	6:50	9:00
Ar. Lake Placid	8:15	12:40	3:05	7:20	

CHAPTER XVI

Good Health, Long Life

Even after Paul Smith had passed his 83rd birthday he was as "sound as a bullet" except for a "little trouble with his heart." His mind was clear and active, and he was as eager to make a trade, and as sharp in a business deal as he had been when half that age.

Uncle Paul rarely took medicines and had very little use for them. To be sure he was real familiar with the "acid phosphates," for he always kept a good supply of them on sale in his store. They were all right for the "other feller," but for himself, he passed them by. He sometimes said, "You can ruin your stomach with medicines. And doctors, if I've *got* to have one, give me one that won't give me any medicine. It's nasty stuff. Why! there's a feller buried over there in the cemetery and it says on his tombstone, 'I was well and thought I would be better; I took physic and here I am.' So, no medicine for me!"

Paul did believe, however, in drinking plenty of good, pure, spring water. And, if he was not feeling just as fit as he thought he ought to, he was very likely to give his "stomach a rest" by prescribing for himself a simple bread and milk diet. In fact, bread and milk was a favorite dish with him. He rarely indulged in the rich and varied foods for which his hotel was famous.

In Uncle Paul's later years he was often brought into a discussion about the wisdom of leaving one's bedroom window open at night. He, as well as a great many others of his day, felt that too much mountain air in one's bedroom at night would certainly not be very good for one. He said that he had "lived in this pure mountain air, clear sunlight, and the fragrance of the northern wood for a great many years," and he seemed to think that made him immune to the need for a "fresh air cure."

It was a glad day for Paul Smith when he realized that he seemed to be completely recovered from his recent long illness. How he hated being sick! It was so good to be really well again, and to have the strength of body to go along with the thoughts and dreams of ways to better conditions in his portion of his beloved Adirondacks.

Long Life in Snow Country

The winter of 1910-11 was a winter of much snow in the north country, and it came on to stay earlier than usual, and buried the Paul Smith Hotel garden before the vegetables were all harvested. About the first of February they ran short of carrots, and regretted that they hadn't gotten them all dug in the fall. Then someone remarked that the ground hadn't been frozen when the snows came. It was after that that some of the hotel crew dug through the deep snow and uncovered a portion of the carrot bed. The carrots proved to be in perfect condition, and much better flavored than the ones they had been using that had been dug in the fall.

The hotel people were no longer short of carrots, nor were they short of snow, for 90 inches of it fell between November 13th and February 11th. When that fact was mentioned, someone was sure to add, "And it is still coming!"

Being told of the digging of the carrots through the snow reminded Uncle Paul that John St. Germain had kept track of the depth of the snowfall at Paul's for a number of years. Just when he began to keep the record is not known, but in February of 1911 he reported that since he had been recording it, the winter of 1902-03 had produced the most snow — 132 inches of the white stuff having fallen that winter.

Paul went on to say that he had spent most of the past 60 winters in the Adirondacks, and he was sure the average depth of the year's fall of snow was gradually getting less. He said that a good share of those earlier winters the snow would reach a depth of 6 or 7 feet on the level; that if a man tried to walk in it, without snowshoes, he would sink into it to his armpits. He talked about what a trial it was living in the woods when the snow was so deep, and there was no way to dispose of, or move, the snow except to shovel it. When the snow was so deep, horses and cattle could not move around in it, and would have to be kept in their stables. A man taking care of them would have to wear snowshoes between buildings. And instead of letting the animals out to water, the water would have to be carried to them.

Paul Smith believed that the shallower depth of snow in the

more recent years was due in some part to the cutting of so much of the timber. "For," said he, "the timber holds the snow."

Paul also went on to tell of something that had happened many years before, in one of those winters of much too much snow.

A woodsman, on snowshoes, from out near McCollom's, had stopped at Paul's for a bit of rest and refreshment. In the course of his visit, he told of seeing tracks where someone had passed some hours before, along the road, or at least where the road was supposed to be. (But in those early days there was not enough travel to keep the roads open, and every new fall of snow would fill and cover the road completely.) The tracks the woodsman had seen had shown that the man was wading in snow more than waist deep. After awhile the trail left the road and went out toward the southern end of Mountain Pond.

As the men at the hotel discussed the episode they agreed that the man must be a stranger to the area, since he was without snowshoes. They also agreed that he might be in desperate trouble because of his inability to travel, and the intense cold.

The men and Paul agreed that the stranger couldn't have gotten very far, and it should be easy to find him by the trail he made. So several of the men took a few blankets on a toboggan and set out to find the traveler and bring him in if it so happened he might need the help.

The men were back in a few hours. They had had no trouble in finding the stranger, but he was already dead. He had gotten only a little way out on the pond before he had sunk down into the snow, and stayed there. They brought him to the hotel, but no one there had ever seen him before. And there was absolutely no identification on him. The body was kept for a number of days, but nothing was ever found out about him. They finally buried him in the Vermontville cemetery. The clothing which he had on at the time of his death was kept for some years in the hope that it would help to identify the stranger if anyone ever came to inquire for him. But no one ever came.

The days, and the weeks, and the months of 1911 went by so speedily. Summer came and rushed on into August, and it was soon the day before Uncle Paul's birthday again. It seemed that in those last few years Paul's birthday made an excellent excuse for old friends, and new, to gather 'round and do honor to this much loved old gentleman of the woods.

The hotel was full of guests and the surrounding camps were overflowing with families and their visitors. That evening the Misses Broadhead of New York City entertained Paul at a small dinner. The main feature of the occasion was a huge and handsome cake with its many candles aglow.

With the appearance of the cake in the spacious dining room, hundreds of friends appeared, seemingly from nowhere, to give the honored guest an ovation. Back-slapping, hand-shaking, greetings and congratulations prevailed for a while. Later on the cake was cut and passed around among those present.

The next day was Sunday and Paul Smith, Jr. and his wife gave a birthday dinner for their father. Among those present were Dr. and Mrs. Edward Livingston Trudeau, who had spent all but one of the past 35 summers at Paul Smith's; Mr. and Mrs. William McAlpin of Camp Windover; and Mrs. Andrew White of Syracuse, who was a guest of Mrs. Paul Smith, Jr.

Paul was showered with good wishes and congratulations in the form of verbal messages, cards, letters and telegrams. Many presents were either sent, or brought to him. Among them was one of Adirondack Murray's books. It was a gift from Sister Mary Kernan of Gabriels Sanatorium. Mrs. I. L. Adams of New York City gave him an interesting clock; and George Stevens of the Stevens House in Lake Placid presented him with a large box of roses. He also received a handsome bouquet of red carnations from Mrs. John Shoiba, of Bala, Pennsylvania, and many other interesting gifts.

Perhaps the most unusual gift was given by Wallace Cosgrove, who was a member of the Paul Smith's Hotel baseball team. He had sent to New York City to obtain a new silver dollar that was minted in 1825 — the year of Paul's birth. Word came back to him that no silver dollars were minted from 1804 to 1832. So Cosgrove ordered two new 1825 silver half-dollars, and gave them instead.

Paul had made pleasant and witty speeches — very characteristic of him — as he gave thanks for each gift. When he thanked Cosgrove for the half-dollars he was all smiles as he said, "I'll carry these with me always. Then I'll always have some money. Before I die I'll put them into two envelopes and leave one to each one of my boys to buy bread with."

And so another year drew to a close for Uncle Paul. Since recovering from his illness of the year before he had been in good health, and at his birthday party was talking of spending a part of the winter in California, which had become an almost unfailing custom during the later years of his life.

The Changing Dream

On a Sunday in early May of 1912 Paul Smith went, with a companion, from his hotel home on the St. Regis Lake to Franklin Falls, traveling along at a great rate of speed.

In spite of the excitement of the speed Paul could not help thinking back over the past — nearly 60 years of it — since he made his first trip over a portion of that road; and to the changes that had taken place during that span of time.

One of the greatest changes was in his mode of travel. On his first trip into the Adirondacks he had no way to travel except to walk, unless chance might offer him a ride on a crude cart behind a yoke of oxen, or less probable, behind a horse, or a team of horses. Whenever those chances came they seemed like the height of luxury.

The road also had changed much, for many a sharp bend had been straightened a bit. A few of the humps had been leveled off to fill some of the hollows; some rocks had been dug out and the holes filled up. Stones had been thrown into low, muddy places, and dirt spread over the, until the roads seemed to be just about all anyone could expect, at least of a wilderness road.

The countryside itself had changed. Where, in the beginning, there had been nothing but mountainous wilderness that was almost completely covered with forests — a clearing of any size at all being very rare to find — now he passed many a modest home, set a bit back from the road, with acres of cleared and cultivated land on all sides.

As he came into Franklin Falls he looked all about and saw the great changes that had taken place there also. The hotel, the Franklin Falls House, where he had wooed, and won, and married his wife, still stood, but it was rapidly coming into disuse, because of less travel passing by its doors. Paul looked at the building with a speculative eye, and thought that perhaps it might be enlarged in usefulness by reconstructing, and modernizing it.

Then he passed on a little farther to the very newest of his projects. It had just been completely finished and he had come to make his first inspection of it. That power plant was another change that Paul Smith was thinking of that morning, for when he had first come into the area there was only a mill there for converting logs into lumber. Now the very latest thing in an electrical power plant stood on the spot. The river above the plant had changed too, for a strong dam had been built across the river, and as soon as the basin was filled to the holding capacity of the dam there would be a beautiful lake where only a river had been before. Paul stood and gazed at it all with pride, and the satisfaction of accomplishment.

As he thought of all these changes he realized that perhaps the greatest change of all had been in himself. He had come into the region as a young man, satisfied with life if he could earn enough to feed and clothe himself while he wandered the woods and fished and hunted to his heart's content. Almost accidentally he began to guide other hunters and fishermen, and found that by so doing he could earn what he needed. And at the same time he was doing what he wanted most to do. The hotel-keeping had also come about almost as an accident as he followed the suggestion of some of the men he guided. The idea that had been given him had grown into proportions never thought of in the beginning.

As all of these thoughts came to him, Paul came to understand why people spoke of him as the "Pioneer Resort Hotel-Keeper in the Adirondacks." He knew that his hotel business *had* been a success — a *great* success; and that in spite of the fact that for so many years his place was so lacking in modern conveniences; no running water, no modern baths, or toilet facilities, no telephone, no electricity, no bellboy service, 40 to 50 miles from the railroad, the place was never wanting for guests during the months it was open. Those who stopped there once were never satisfied unless they returned again, and often.

Paul saw that his own development and success had somehow come to pass right along with the change and the progress of the country. He, who had come into the area without owning a foot of land, and with scarcely a dollar in his pocket, had come into the ownership of so much. He stood and looked again at the Franklin Falls Hotel that had seemed such a grand modern House in the days when he and Lydia were married. He owned it, and the river banks, the water power, and hundreds of acres on both sides of the river; and for many miles both up and down stream from the spot where he was standing. He also owned a power plant at Union Falls, several miles down stream from Franklin Falls, together with hundred of acres of land along the river between the two power plants. And all this was only a small part of his possessions.

Perhaps the greatest change in Paul Smith was that in the beginning he seemed to many to be indolent, lazy, a dreamer, rather than one who wanted to *do*. But as the years had passed his ideas and dreams had certainly kept him active, and *doing*. He was *still* at it; for even as he stood there near his new plant he was thinking of the next one, and said to his companion, "It is a wonderful plant! A perfect plant! But we'll build another one some day at Shell Rock which will be as far advanced over this one as this one is over any of the others."

It was ever so with Paul Smith. When one idea grew and became a success, a new idea almost always came to take its place to be worked out.

So Paul Smith *had* changed. It spite of his age, there were no more indolent dreamy periods for him. Life was full to the brim. He was still mentally alert, and planning much for the future, instead of being satisfied to sit down and live in the past.

But there was one way in which Paul *didn't* change, and that was in his enjoyment of a joke. Through the years, as each power plant was built, it was the most modern of its time. In spite of that, there would fairly often be an interruption in the transmitting of the electricity, and the lights would suddenly go out, usually for only a few seconds. When some guest would always answer, "Oh! It's nothing much! Just a trout in the wheel probably. It will be out in a minute." And it most always happened that the lights would soon be back on.

By now Paul had become an international figure, and was referred to the world over simply as "Uncle Paul." His hotel had been built up and added to with all the modern facilities available. The hotel itself had 225 rooms (nearly all with its own bath) and with the surrounding cottages that were under their control, the Smiths could take care of more than 500 guests.

CHAPTER XVII

We Knew Him Well

The days of 1912 sped quickly by until August 19th came along. It, of course, was the day before Uncle Paul's birthday, and he decided to celebrate early by going to the circus. It seemed to him a good way for any boy, young or old, to spend a day It is quite likely that Paul had not been to the circus for quite a number of years. Probably not since the days when his old friend, Phineas Taylor Barnum, had owned it. And, on that August day, it proved to be a mistake for him to go; for whatever joy or fun he may have gotten out of the circus was offset by his almost overpowering desire to see, and commune with his old friend, Barnum, who had died in 1891. It left him with a feeling of sadness that was very hard for him to throw off.

The next day was his birthday. But neither birthday nor sad heart could keep Paul from looking after his car-rental business as usual. So he made his regular inspection of cars, visited here and there, and then went with a friend on an inspection tour of his Franklin Falls electric plant.

The trip itself was delightful as they traveled by automobile, and now and then when the road was especially good reached the then great speed of 40 miles an hour. To Paul this plant seemed one of his greatest achievements, and he took great delight and pride in it as well he might. For in the course of time the Paul Smith's Electric Light and Power Company were supplying power to Bloomingdale, Saranac Lake, Tupper Lake, Paul Smith's Gabriels, Lake Clear, Onchiota, Merrillsville, Loon Lake, Vermontville, Ausable Forks and to all the out-lying areas in and around and about these communities.

The next day Uncle Paul was again given a birthday party. But perhaps it might be termed more of a birthday dinner than a party. This time it was to honor his 87th birthday. As in other years he received scores of telegrams, cards and letters, many gifts

179

and hundreds of personal congratulations. The St. Regis region was filled with summer visitors, many of them having as their main reason for being in the area at that time their desire to be present at Uncle Paul's birthday celebration. Everyone present enjoyed the festivity, none of them realizing that this would be the last birthday party for Uncle Paul.

It was not long after that 87th birthday that Uncle Paul became ill. His sons and friends were quite alarmed about his condition; especially so as they thought of his age. And, although all through his life Paul had very little regard, almost a contempt, for the abilities of doctors, it became necessary to call one in. It soon became apparent that Uncle Paul needed more help than the local doctors were able to give him, so, on October 17th, his sons took him to the Royal Victoria Hospital in Montreal. There it soon developed that Paul needed an operation. But due to his age, and to a little trouble he had with his heart some time before, the doctors were hesitant about advising it. However, as they studied the situation, they found that for many years Paul had been a "careful eater," never over eating of any food, and almost invariably choosing the simple and plain foods, reverting to them more and more as time went on. He was more fond of a bowl of bread and milk than of any other food.

The doctors also found that Paul Smith had never been a heavy smoker or drinker, though he had had both habits in moderation until the age of 85 when he completely quit each of them. His background of good health and clean living, and the very great need determined the doctor's decision, and the operation was performed. It has been spoken of by some as a kidney operation, by others as a gall bladder operation. The gall bladder operation seems more plausible, but it is difficult to determine now.

The courageous old man came through that operation famously, but the need for a second operation soon developed and was performed a few weeks later. From that Paul was unable to rally, and he died in the hospital.

Phelps and Paul brought their father home about noon on a Monday. They placed him in the parlor of their own cottage home, there to remain until shortly after noon on Wednesday when a short prayer was said before taking him the short distance to the little church, "St. John's in the Wilderness." (That lovely little church which Paul had given so much toward the building.) There the funeral service was held at 2:30 p.m., December 18, 1912.

It was the largest funeral ever to be held in northern New York, up to that time, at least. Between 700 and 800 people were present, and they came from far and near, and from all walks of life; young and old, rich and poor, white and black, they were all there. Floral tributes, telegrams and letters of condolence poured in from prominent people in all parts of the world. Few men in private life have ever been laid to rest with more out-pourings of esteem than were granted to Paul Smith — no man deserved them more. Burial was in the family plot in the cemetery close by.

The Rev. William Brown Lusk officiated at the service. He chose his text from Job 14: 7 & 10: "For there is hope of a tree, if it be cut down, that it will sprout again . . . But man dieth, and wasteth away: yea, man giveth up the ghost."

Bearers were John J. Flanagan, A. B. Banker, E. C. Pine, O. S. Lawrence, W. H. Anderson, and John Harding. Honorary bearers were James M. Bell, Frank D. Kilburn, J. H. Moffitt, Thos. Cantwell, Geo. A. Stevens, Robert J. Clarke, Wallace Murray and John Roberts.

Every newspaper in the state, and many others throughout the world carried his obituary, and most of them had something extra to add about Paul Smith, the man, such as, "He hewed his fortune and his fame out of the primeval wilderness, and he compassed the former without tarnishing the latter. He lived and died, respected and loved by both old and young, rich and poor alike. In the early days of his hotel, his name is said to have been more frequently spoken than any other in the state. I have heard the name of Paul Smith fall from the lips of high and low for many years, but I have never heard it coupled with malice or reproach."

Paul had a "good word for everybody. No matter how humble, the poor received as much consideration as the aristocrats . . . and this was what made him so popular. He liked to be talked to; would stand with one foot extended, favoring his lame hip . . . his thumb caught in the armhole of his vest, with one eye partly closed as he took on that shrewd look of his, and looked one right in the eye. When he was listening to a tale of woe he sympathized, while, if it was a story of good luck, he appeared as pleased as though it concerned himself."

"Although he had great wealth, had a post office, express office, railway stations, palace cars, and steamboats named after him, he remained the same Paul Smith and never got lofty ideas as most men would have done. He liked to talk of the days of when he first came from Vermont a poor man. A stranger would never believe that he possessed great wealth, and was on intimate terms with many of the richest and most prominent people in the country. Through his death the country lost a great man."

Paul Smith was truly a pioneer, a son of the forest; a great many of his accomplishments came about, and were worked out, because he was as he sometimes said, "Born Smart."

References

Adirondack Daily Enterprise, July 11, 1912; August 22, 1912; July 17, 1913.

Collins, Geraldine, *The Biography and Funny Sayings of Paul Smith,* Paul Smith's College, 1965.

DeSormo, Maitland, *The Heydays of the Adirondacks*, Adirondack Yesteryears, 1974.

Donaldson, Alfred L., "Paul Smith" from *A History of the Adirondacks*. Century, New York 1921. Reprinted by Harbor Hill Books.

"Forest Leaves," Quarterly magazine published by Gabriels Sanitorium, Vol. 1-a, December, 1903.

Journal of the Outdoor Life, 1925.

Long, E., *Funny Sayings of the Late Paul Smith*.

Longtin, R., "Paul Smith," paper, January 30, 1957.

Porter, Marjorie L., "Paul Smith" from *North Country Life*, Fall, 1951.

Porter, Marjorie Lansing. *Lem Merrill, Surveryor, Conservationist*, Clinton Press, Plattsburgh, 1944.

Saranac Lake Free Library, Scrapbook clippings about Paul Smith.

Titus, John H., *Adirondack Pioneers*, Troy Times Press, 1899.

Trudeau, Edward Livingston, M.D., *An Autobiography*, Doubleday Page, Garden City, 1915.